Getting
Naked

Also by Patrick Lencioni

Leadership Fables

The Five Temptations of a CEO

The Four Obsessions of an Extraordinary Executive

The Five Dysfunctions of a Team

Death by Meeting

Silos, Politics, and Turf Wars

The Three Signs of a Miserable Job

The Three Big Questions for a Frantic Family

Field Guide

Overcoming the Five Dysfunctions of a Team

Getting Naked

A BUSINESS FABLE ABOUT SHEDDING THE THREE FEARS THAT SABOTAGE CLIENT LOYALTY

Patrick Lencioni

JOSSEY-BASS
A Wiley Imprint
www.josseybass.com

Published by Jossey-Bass
A Wiley Imprint
989 Market Street, San Francisco, CA 94103-1741—www.josseybass.com

Readers should be aware that Internet Web sites offered as citations and/or sources for further information may have changed or disappeared between the time this was written and when it is read.

Limit of Liability/Disclaimer of Warranty: While the publisher and author have used their best efforts in preparing this book, they make no representations or warranties with respect to the accuracy or completeness of the contents of this book and specifically disclaim any implied warranties of merchantability or fitness for a particular purpose. No warranty may be created or extended by sales representatives or written sales materials. The advice and strategies contained herein may not be suitable for your situation. You should consult with a professional where appropriate. Neither the publisher nor author shall be liable for any loss of profit or any other commercial damages, including but not limited to special, incidental, consequential, or other damages.

Jossey-Bass books and products are available through most bookstores. To contact Jossey-Bass directly call our Customer Care Department within the U.S. at 800-956-7739, outside the U.S. at 317-572-3986, or fax 317-572-4002.

Jossey-Bass also publishes its books in a variety of electronic formats. Some content that appears in print may not be available in electronic books.

Library of Congress Cataloging-in-Publication Data
Lencioni, Patrick, 1965-
  Getting naked : a business fable about shedding the three fears that sabotage client loyalty / Patrick Lencioni.
    p. cm.
  ISBN 978-0-7879-7639-2 (cloth)
  1. Customer loyalty. 2. Customer relations. I. Title.
  HF5415.525L46 2010
  658.8'12—dc22
                                                                    2009046010

Printed in the United States of America
FIRST EDITION
HB Printing   10 9 8 7 6 5 4 3 2 1

CONTENTS

This book is dedicated to all The Table Group consulting partners around the world who are practicing naked service with clients every day.

INTRODUCTION

Vulnerability. It is one of the most undervalued and misunderstood of all human qualities.

Without the willingness to be vulnerable, we will not build deep and lasting relationships in life. That's because there is no better way to earn a person's trust than by putting ourselves in a position of unprotected weakness and demonstrating that we believe they will support us.

Yet society encourages us to avoid vulnerability, to always project strength, confidence, and poise. Although this is certainly advisable in some situations in life, when it comes to important, ongoing relationships, it stifles our ability to build trust.

For those who provide service to clients, vulnerability is particularly powerful. Those who get comfortable being vulnerable—or as I call it, naked—are rewarded with levels of client loyalty and intimacy that other service providers can only dream of.

Whenever I explain this to an audience, I am often asked, "But can't you be too vulnerable?" Surprisingly, the answer is no. Of course, if you come to your clients every day admitting that you've made yet another mistake or that you don't know how to do yet another required element of your job, that would be a serious problem. But it would be not an issue of vulnerability, but rather of competence; the problem would not lie in the *admitting* of so many weaknesses, but in the *having* of them!

Which reminds me of the flaw in that old adage *never let them see you sweat*. The truth is, our clients almost always know when we are sweating, often before we do. And so we have a choice. We can either pretend we're not sweaty and try to hide our weaknesses, and then watch our credibility erode. Or we can raise up our arms, acknowledge our sweatiness, and show them that we are honest and self-assured enough to be worthy of their trust.

If this is so simple in theory—and I'll be the first to admit that it is—then why do we so often resist being naked with clients?

For one, we think it will hurt our chances for success. We fail to realize that, even though clients require us to be competent enough to meet their needs, it is ultimately our honesty, humility, and selflessness that will endear us to them and allow them to trust and depend on us.

But even if we come to understand this on an intellectual level, most of us will still struggle with vulnerability because we are human beings who don't like to be weak, which means we are subject to the completely natural but irrational fears that make us uncomfortable being naked. This book is about overcoming those fears, which is not easy. It requires levels of self-sacrifice and discomfort—and, at times, real suffering—that few people are willing to endure.

So naked service is rare, which means it provides an opportunity for a powerful and tangible competitive advantage for those who embrace it. They will build stronger, stickier relationships with their clients; they'll have an easier time getting those clients to actively and enthusiastically recommend and endorse them, even without being asked; they'll have more comfortable and collaborative discussions about pricing and fees; and they'll enjoy their work much more.

But more than any of that, what makes naked service worthwhile is that it puts us in a position to more effectively help our clients, which, of course, is what providing service is all about. It is my hope that this little book helps you understand how to do just that.

Okay. Now it's time to get naked.

Getting
Naked

The Fable

PART ONE

Theory

ENEMIES

Ican't say that I hated Michael Casey.

For one, Sister Rose Marie Hennessey had taught me in second grade that I should never hate anyone. And besides, I had never actually met Casey. I don't think you can really hate someone you haven't met, even if you ignore Sister Rose Marie's advice.

But I'm not going to lie; Michael Casey was one of my least favorite people in the world. Even the mention of his name could put me in a moderately bad mood.

And so, if you had told me a year earlier that I would spend four solid months of my professional life learning about him and his annoying little consulting firm, I would have told you it was time for me to change careers.

But that's exactly what happened, and I've lived to tell about it.

ME

I'm Jack Bauer, and yes, I share a name with that guy on TV who saved the world every year. Unlike him, though, I'm not a superhero. I'm just a consultant.

For five years I'd been working within the strategy practice at Kendrick and Black, a prestigious, international full-service management consulting firm headquartered in San Francisco.

In addition to being one of the senior consultants in our division, I headed up sales for the strategy practice of our firm. This meant I sometimes competed for clients with Michael Casey and his firm, Lighthouse Partners.

Now, Lighthouse was a much smaller firm than ours, and they focused most of their work in the Bay Area, so we didn't run up against them in more than 5 or 10 percent of the projects that we pursued. But when we did, we lost every single time.

That's not exactly true. We won once. But a year later the client, a small start-up called DecisionTech, threw us out and hired Lighthouse, which was more painful than losing to them in the first place. What was especially painful was the fact that all of these losses occurred in our own backyard, providing particularly high-profile defeats for all of our local peers to see. This only exacerbated our bitterness toward Michael Casey.

Keep in mind that, unlike in the world of sports, when you compete against a consulting firm you almost never actually see your competitors. But you hear about them. And after listening to story after story about how amazing and smart and effective Michael Casey and his team were, I would have liked nothing more than to hear they were going out of business.

Or so I thought.

HORRIBLE
PROMOTION

When I was first told by a colleague that Michael Casey was leaving Lighthouse and that his firm was for sale, I was ecstatic. We had finally worn him down, I decided. There was a chink in their armor after all; no one could be that good.

When I learned that he was leaving to "spend more time with his family," my euphoria diminished a little, but not much. Spending more time with your family was one of the most commonly used phrases for papering over a performance issue. Regardless of the reason, Lighthouse was up for sale and we wouldn't have to compete with and be humiliated by them ever again.

My glee at hearing about the demise of my enemy came to an abrupt end five days later when the founder of our firm, Jim Kendrick, pulled the rug out from under me.

Keep in mind that Jim had stopped by my office only twice before. Once to formally welcome me to his firm. Another time to warn me not to screw up a project for one of our biggest clients. He wasn't known for being overly warm or tactful.

"Here's the deal, Jack. You probably know about a little consulting firm over in Half Moon Bay called Lighthouse Partners."

"Yeah, I know them." I said it like I had never given them a second thought.

He continued, "Well, they were desperate to be sold in a hurry, and Marty said they were probably worth the risk. So we bought them before anyone else could. And so I wanted to—"

I was shocked and felt suddenly threatened, which is probably why, before he could finish, I interrupted: "What are we going to do with them?"

"We . . ." He paused, smiling a little condescendingly at my impatience. " . . . are going to have you manage it for a while. We want you to spend five or six months overseeing the firm, which shouldn't take more than half of your daily hours. As soon as you get your hands around what's going on over there, we can integrate whatever parts of it we decide to keep into our strategy division, and figure out what to do with the rest. And if all goes well, you should be heading the strategy division by then, given that Marty will be retiring next summer." He paused as if he were simply out of words. "Okay then." And he left.

Just like that, my world had been turned upside down, and for the rest of the day I couldn't decide how to digest it all. As I explained to my wife that night, I should have been happy. But there was something about the situation that made me uncomfortable.

Part of it was certainly the realization that if this went poorly, my career would be considerably damaged—and that

I'd have Lighthouse Partners to thank for it. Michael Casey just might continue to haunt me even after his departure.

Another reason for my discomfort was the thought of having to finally meet the man, to sit down with him face-to-face to discuss the transition.

As it turned out, that would not happen.

ACCELERATION

Casey's departure from Lighthouse turned out to be more abrupt than anyone expected. As soon as the ink was dry on the deal, he was gone.

I was relieved by this, but less than I would have expected, probably because I was suddenly suspicious about whether there was something wrong at the firm.

When I asked my boss, Marty, about the circumstances, he shrugged. "I don't know. It happened so fast, we had very little time for any due diligence. But for Kendrick, the cost was relatively low, and for some reason he thought it was worth the risk."

I sensed Marty wasn't telling me the whole story. "Come on—you were the one pushing hard for the deal, weren't you?"

Marty smiled. "Maybe."

"So how are these people feeling about the whole thing?"

Marty shrugged. "I really have no idea. But you'll probably find out on Wednesday."

"Wednesday?"

"Yeah." Marty grinned. "You're meeting with the partners over at Lighthouse Wednesday morning."

Marty was a wiry, well-dressed fifty-seven-year-old work-aholic who had suddenly decided he was ready for early retirement and a chance at unlimited golf. And evidently he never had a Sister Rose Marie in second grade, because out of nowhere he remarked, "I really hate Michael Casey."

Unlike me, Marty had actually met the man on a few occasions, and considering it was his division that Lighthouse had been beating up on for the past dozen years, I suppose his hatred could be at least partly justified.

"Phony," "falsely modest," and "self-righteous" were the terms Marty used to describe Casey. I can't deny that Marty's feelings influenced me—or more accurately, infected me—and encouraged my hostility toward our rival. But I didn't like losing any more than Marty did, so I had nurtured my own bitterness toward the man and his little firm during my five years at Kendrick and Black.

"What's your hypothesis about how all of this is going to pan out?" I wanted to know.

Marty took a breath and thought about it for a second. "It's hard to say for sure. But I'll tell you this: I don't see too many of their partners making it through the next year."

"Why do you say that?"

"I don't know." As he thought about it, he winced. "More than anything else, we just have two completely different cultures."

I wasn't surprised by his comment, but I wanted a little more in terms of specifics. "For instance?"

This time he didn't hesitate. "From what I hear, the place is a country club."

Marty could see that I didn't understand what he meant, so he explained. "They've got this funky office that used to be a kindergarten or preschool or something like that. I hear that their parking lot is empty by seven o'clock every night. They don't work weekends. Ever. It's a playground. Their partners would get eaten alive here."

"Isn't that a problem for us?"

Marty shook his head and smiled. "Not really. We'll get their clients and the consultants who do all the real work. That's the reason we did the deal in the first place."

I was starting to get a little nervous. "So, why don't you come with me Wednesday?"

Marty's eyes went wide. "Oh, I'd love to."

I was relieved, until he continued, "But Kendrick and I agreed that this is something you need to do on your own. At least for now." He paused. "But if you don't come back and give me a detailed, blow-by-blow account of the meetings, and a vivid and dramatic description of every detail about that damn company, I'll fire you."

We laughed. Or at least he did. I was probably a little distracted, thinking about what would be coming on Wednesday.

BAND-AIDS

As a consultant, I had always advised my clients who acquired companies to accelerate the transitions and integrations, to avoid letting problems linger or fester. "Ripping the Band-Aid off quickly" is how I liked to characterize it. But now that I was the one doing the integrating and ripping, I was starting to question that advice. Still, I had no choice.

So, forty-eight hours after the contract had been signed, I found myself driving west along the crooked highway connecting the San Francisco Bay Area to the coastal town of Half Moon Bay. That's where the twenty-five employees of Lighthouse Partners were waiting to hear what I had to say about their future. They could not have been more curious than I was.

The Lighthouse office was not exactly what Marty had described. But it was darn close.

Standing alone and apart from the rest of the small agricultural town was a tiny campus of sorts, with four rectangular buildings separated by breezeways and small, neatly manicured lawns. It had certainly once been a school of some kind (I would later learn that it had been an elementary school for the developmentally disabled who were now being mainstreamed into the school system). Today it was the home of three companies: a small wine distributor, an agricultural supply sales office, and Lighthouse Partners.

After parking my car in what had once been a playground, I immediately saw why Michael Casey had chosen the name for his company. No more than a quarter of a mile to the west was a small but unmistakable lighthouse, mostly white with three equally spaced blue stripes. I wondered why so many people, including me, liked lighthouses so much.

The school building reminded me of my own grammar school, except that this one had been spruced up and redecorated to look somewhat corporate. I was surprised—and, I'll admit, somehow pleased—to see that the bathrooms in the center of the building still had "Boys" and "Girls" signs on the outside, and that an old-fashioned drinking fountain with three separate spigots was mounted on the wall between them. I couldn't help but think about Sister Rose Marie.

Walking the corridor, I found a door with a Lighthouse sign on it and went inside.

PART TWO

Practice

CONTACT

The inside of the building did not match the exterior. A reception area and a large, fishbowl-like conference room dominated the front part of the building, which had been redone in brick and simple wood. The rest of the building and, as I would later learn, another across the quad, had been converted into open office areas. Everything was neat and simple, with desks and bookshelves along the walls, and skylights everywhere.

I was greeted by a petite, fortyish blonde woman in blue jeans who was sitting at the front desk. "Can I help you?"

Before I could answer, she continued, "Are you Jack?" Though she apparently knew who I was, she smiled politely as though I were just another visitor, maybe the FedEx guy or a caterer, but certainly not the conquering general arriving to size up the spoils of his victory.

"I'm here for a meeting with Amy Stirling and Dick Janice." I'm pretty sure that I didn't smile, because I felt a sudden surge of self-consciousness and inferiority. I wondered if she noticed.

Without a trace of anxiety, she responded, "I'm Amy Stirling."

Like a moron, I spoke without thinking, asking a question that was as unnecessary as it was inane. "Is this where you sit, Amy?"

She smiled in a puzzled kind of way. "No, this is the reception desk. Christa is on her honeymoon, so we're all trying to cover for her. And I was waiting for you."

Seeming to sense my discomfort, Amy continued, "Why don't you go on into the conference room, and I'll see if I can't find Dick and Matt. Grab a drink from the kitchen if you want something." She motioned to a doorway next to the conference room.

A minute later I was sitting alone at the oak table in the fishbowl room, opening a Diet Coke. And then it dawned on me.

So this is it. This is the physical source of the frustration and anxiety that Marty and I have been feeling.

Suddenly, I had an urge to get up and explore every nook and cranny of the office, to invisibly observe the meetings and listen in on the phone calls where they plotted to drive us crazy. That impulse was quickly and strangely replaced by an urge to leave.

I couldn't decide whether I was more afraid of confronting the little monster I had been loathing for these past few years, or of discovering that it wasn't as ugly as I had imagined. Whatever the case, it was too late to consider, because at that moment Amy and two of her colleagues walked into the room.

Q&A

Dick Janice, the oldest of the partners and someone whose name I had heard a few times in the course of my sales adventures, greeted me first. He was a bigger, balder man than I had expected, in good shape for someone who looked to be half way between fifty and sixty years old. His handshake was a firm one, which didn't surprise me. Anyone under the age of seventy who hadn't changed his name from Dick back to Richard would have to be fairly tough, I figured.

Dick seemed as friendly and calm as Amy, which I found disturbing all over again. Do these people even know who I am and why I'm here?

Fortunately, the last and youngest of the partners, Matt O'Connor, gave me a nervous vibe that reconnected me with reality. A freckle-faced redhead, Matt didn't manage to smile when he shook my hand, and he looked away as soon as he could.

Dick spoke first. "Welcome to Half Moon Bay, Jack. I hope you didn't have any problem finding our strange little office."

I assured him I hadn't, and we exchanged a few pleasantries about the weather and the blue-striped lighthouse and the school building where they worked. Then I decided to take control of the discussion.

"Okay, so how are you guys doing?" I didn't give them a chance to answer. "Things must be a little unsettling right now."

I was afraid they were going to look at me as though they didn't know what I was talking about and say "No, actually we're good."

Thankfully, they didn't. Dick went first, smiling painfully. "I'd say things are at an all-time low from a morale standpoint."

The others nodded, but Amy clarified. "It's not that anyone's going to jump out a window or anything. They're just in shock, and a little worried. But they're busy, and that's good."

"How is business these days?" I asked. Before they could respond, I felt the need to clarify. "I mean, normally I would have all that information before coming in here today. But I just found out about all this two days ago and I've been traveling, so—"

Dick interrupted, reassuringly: "Don't worry about it. We're all spinning a little right now."

Finally, Matt spoke, in a slightly defensive tone. "We're busier than we've been in a long time, and we're completely maxed out in terms of bandwidth. We had to turn down two clients this month, good clients, because we just couldn't handle the load. But just this morning we reluctantly agreed to work with a new client, and that's going to be a push for us until a few people get back from vacation."

Though I'm sure that I concealed my surprise, I couldn't believe what I was hearing.

At K&B, we had never turned down a client, not if they could pay us. Even if we were strapped for consultants, we would borrow someone from another practice, accelerate our hiring, or, more often than not, just work people that much harder into the evening and on weekends. This must have been what Marty was referring to when he talked about the country club.

"Well, it's great that you're busy." I tried my best to seem sincere, but I realized that I probably came across as patronizing. Whatever. "By the way, who is your new client?"

Amy responded first. "A supply chain company in San Mateo called Boxcar."

This time I had to work even harder to hide my reaction.

Boxcar had been one of the potential clients in our sales pipeline, and I had them rated pretty high in terms of our probability of closing them. I hadn't known they were even talking to Lighthouse.

As much as I wanted to ask about how they won the deal, I didn't want to acknowledge my own loss. I decided to let it go and change the subject.

"So, how much do you know about Kendrick and Black?"

Amy went first. "Well, I know you're headquartered in the city, and that you're a lot bigger than we are. But to be honest, I don't really know a lot about how you guys approach the market and how you work with clients. I'm assuming that you have a variety of different practices, but I couldn't say what they are and how you compare to any of the other big consulting firms out there. They all kind of blend together for me."

I have to admit that I didn't believe her for a second. As a partner, she had to know more than that about one of her biggest competitors.

Matt chimed in before I could fill in the blanks for Amy. "You know, five or six years ago I sat next to someone on an airplane who worked in the Human Capital practice at K&B. I remember her telling me that you," he directed his remarks at me, "have four or five offices around the country, and something like five different practices."

I politely corrected him. "We've grown the number of offices to seven, one in London and another in Beijing, and consolidated our practices down to four. There's strategy, which is my practice. Human capital, which includes HR and team-building and organizational stuff. Finance, which includes everything from mergers and acquisitions to investments. And M&O—manufacturing and operations—which I suppose is pretty self-explanatory."

Matt was writing all of this down as though he really had no idea.

"What's the culture at K&B like?" Dick asked.

"Well, it's very collegial and professional and client-focused," I responded without even thinking.

"How so?" Dick wanted to know.

"Well, I hoped you weren't going to ask that, because I don't really know what any of that means. We just say it because it's printed in our brochures and on our website."

Actually, I didn't say that. Instead, I gave him some generic pitch about working together across disciplines and going the extra mile for clients, blah blah blah. Frankly, I wasn't sure there really was a culture at K&B, other than doing whatever you had to do to keep your clients happy and paying their bills. And to me, that seemed like the best kind of culture for a consulting firm.

"What about you?" Amy asked. "How long have you been there? What is your role at the firm?"

I was actually starting to believe that she really didn't know anything about me, my firm, or what was going on here. If I had been in her shoes, sitting on the wrong side of a merger, I'd have tapped into every resource this side of the CIA to find out who and what and why things were happening. She seemed to be just going along for the ride.

"Well, I head up sales for our strategy practice. I've been at K&B for a little more than five years. Before that I served as a VP of strategic planning for a big medical device company. And before that I was at business school in Boston." I paused, then embarrassed myself when I felt the need to add, "At Harvard."

They seemed genuinely interested and gracious, even when I did my academic name-dropping.

Without changing his facial expression or tone of voice, Dick asked the sixty-four-thousand-dollar question: "So, what do you guys plan to do with us, anyway?"

And there it was.

BRASS TACKS

Paused, but not in an awkward way. If I had come to this meeting prepared to answer any question, it was this one. "That depends. Obviously we didn't acquire you without having a healthy respect for what you do. And in this business, people are your only asset, so I don't think your employees should be worried about anything."

I should have felt worse for giving such a vague and empty, if not downright dishonest, answer. But isn't that what companies say to the firms they acquire?

I wasn't about to tell him how Marty felt about their firm. And I certainly didn't mention that one of the most likely reasons they had been acquired was to remove a thorn from our side and add to our client list. If that were in fact the case, it would become evident soon enough, so there was no reason to make this initial phase of the integration more difficult than it already was.

Now Amy dove in, and her demeanor seemed to change in a subtle but unmistakable way. She was suddenly confident, if not just slightly aggressive. "Jack, how much do you know about us?"

I felt threatened. I stammered. "Well, you guys have a good reputation, as far as I can tell." I wanted to be complimentary but without giving them too much credit and losing my authority. "I know you do most of your work in high tech, and so a lot of it is local."

They nodded and seemed to be waiting for more details. When she realized that I had nothing else to offer, Amy dove back in.

"Okay, you're right that most of our clients are here in the Bay Area, but they're not exclusively high tech. We focus on local clients because years ago Michael Casey decided that there was plenty of work in this area to keep us busy and off of airplanes. So we travel only in rare and special circumstances."

That was the first mention of the famous Mr. Casey, and I wasn't going to do or say anything that would provoke more discussion of him. I wasn't ready for that yet.

So I decided to ask a deflective question. "Your work is exclusively in strategy, am I right?"

Matt shot back, "No. We actually do a lot more than strategy."

Dick smiled and explained, "We market ourselves as a strategy firm, but we almost always end up doing more, usually in the areas of organizational development and operational consulting."

This was news to me. "So once you get a new client and prove yourselves, you sell other projects to them?"

Amy squinted. "Well, I don't think that's how we describe it. It's usually just a matter of clients asking us to take on different projects, and so we've developed something of a competency in those areas. But we don't really advertise any of that, because it really begins and ends with strategy."

As much as I wanted to write all of this down, I didn't want to come across as being too interested or surprised.

Then we were interrupted by a young woman wearing jeans and a sweatshirt who carried a stack of binders into the room and set them on the table. Amy introduced her as Mary, one of the junior consultants at the firm, and she went on her way.

I picked up one of the binders, saw that it contained financial information and client records, and started to get excited. I love data, and I had a feeling that the meeting was about to get fun.

DISCOVERY

ick explained the documents on the table in front of us. "We thought you might want to see our books. We've got a list of our clients, what kind of work we're doing, how much time we spend with each of them, and a basic breakdown of our fees and our costs."

For the next half hour we tore through the binders, diving into the areas that were interesting to me. It would be an understatement to say that I was stunned by what I saw.

First, their client list was much stronger than I had expected. A shorter list than ours, without a doubt, but in some ways a more impressive one, I had to admit. But only to myself.

Their costs per client were slightly higher than ours, which I quickly learned was caused by the fact that they had very few junior consultants. In fact, their average consultant salary was considerably higher than ours, even though they paid their partners less than we did. Lighthouse simply had no legion of young, underpaid worker bees like we had at K&B.

Given their cost structure, I assumed that their profit margins would be lower than ours. This would seem to be inevitable. That's why I had to look twice when I found the page on profitability. They were actually doing a little better than us!

"I'm afraid this doesn't add up," I said out loud—and immediately regretted. "According to these numbers, you guys make about three to five percent more profit per client than we do. That seems impossible!"

Amy and Matt turned the pages in their binders to the same one that I was looking at.

Dick was staring at me, as though he were trying to read my mind. "Why does that seem impossible?"

"I don't know," I stammered. "I mean, if you don't use junior consultants, which leads you to have a higher salary structure than we do, which leads you to have a higher cost basis than we do, then the only way you could be making that much more than we are is if you—"

I don't know if I paused or if she interrupted me. In any case, Amy finished my sentence: "If we charge higher fees?"

"Right," I said, confident that this would be impossible. Kendrick and Black was a prestigious firm, and we were known, even criticized at times by clients, for charging so much for our services.

As I turned through the binder looking for a section on revenue and fees, I kept talking. "Granted, we probably have a little more overhead, but not enough to explain—"

This time no one had to interrupt me. I stopped in mid-sentence as I found the page with the firm's fee structure. Not realizing that I was actually saying what I was thinking, I quietly blurted out, "No way."

"Is something wrong?" Dick seemed genuinely concerned.

It took me a while to realize he had asked me a question. "Wrong? No. No. It's just, well, do you guys actually charge your clients those rates?"

Amy took my binder to confirm what I was reading. "Let me see. Um, no. This isn't right."

I was relieved. Then she explained.

"We changed this last month. Our fees should be about seven percent higher."

Normally I would have played it cool and found a way to disguise my amazement and save face for myself and my company. But the cat was already out of the bag. "You have got to be sh--ting me!"

They smiled, which I took to be a mixture of amusement at my language and pride that I was impressed. "Yeah," Dick confirmed. "That's what we charge."

I had already started digging a hole, and I wasn't in a position to stop shoveling. "Don't your clients complain? I mean, these rates are really high."

The three of them seemed genuinely puzzled.

Matt fielded this one. "Not really. I mean, sure, sometimes a client will tell us they can't afford us. That's a reality in any business. But generally they're fine with our fee structure."

Amy finished the thought. "And once we've worked to build a relationship with them, they almost never mention it."

I cannot deny that it was at that moment that I started to get angry inside. Why, I don't know. Looking back, I suppose it was jealousy, but at the time, it felt like they were rubbing salt in my wounds, reminding me how much better they were than me, than my firm.

I tried to back off and save face at the same time. "Well, obviously there are some other things going on here that explain all this. And there is probably room here for you guys to reduce your cost structure."

I could tell they were suddenly dumbfounded. And I knew what they were thinking. *You think we're overpaid? You want to cut salaries?*

It was as though any goodwill we had built up so far during our meeting had vaporized in that moment. But before they could say anything, two employees started to come into the room, followed by a trickle of others.

Amy looked up at the clock. "Oh, it's already ten-thirty. We're having our employee meeting." She looked at me and said without enthusiasm, "We were hoping you could speak to everyone."

This was not going to be good.

GASOLINE ON A FIRE

In a matter of minutes, the room filled up with somewhere close to twenty people. I don't remember exactly how many there were or even what they looked like, because, frankly, I was reeling. Having lost the support of the three partners, I had this strange feeling as though the khaki-clad employees were a mob of angry townspeople with torches and pitchforks, coming to destroy a beast.

Well, if I was going to be a beast, I would be a good one, I decided.

When the gathered employees had settled down, Dick began. "Thanks for coming, everyone. We thought it would be a good idea to have Jack Bauer " He turned toward me—as a few barely audible chuckles came from those who noted that I share the name of the well-known television character—and went on, "introduce himself and tell us a little about what we can expect in the next few months."

And with that he turned to give me the floor.

"Thanks, Dick. Yes, I'm Jack Bauer, but not the super-agent on TV." No one laughed. I had used that line with clients and employees and strangers on the rental car shuttle a thousand times, and I'd always elicited an appreciative reaction. Today, nothing.

Fine, if that's how they're going to be ...

"I'm one of the senior partners at Kendrick and Black, and I work in the strategy practice there. I'm going to be assuming the responsibility of overseeing Lighthouse and figuring out how to integrate you all into K&B."

A hand went up in the back of the room. One of the torch-bearing townspeople, a guy in a sport coat.

"What do you mean by integrate?"

"Well, let me be clear about something. We did not purchase your firm because we think you're broken. Obviously, you're doing something very well."

I didn't notice any sense of relief among the townspeople. I might as well have been droning on like one of the grown-ups on the *Charlie Brown* TV specials. Still, I continued.

"But with any acquisition, in order to achieve synergies, you make some adjustments to ensure that you're aligning your assets in the way that maximizes your potential." Even *I* thought that sounded like consultant speak.

Another hand went up, this time from a woman with a pitchfork. "Why isn't one of our partners running Lighthouse during the transition?"

The room went cold and silent.

I lurched for comic relief. "Well, first of all I'd like to ask you all to be a little more direct. It seems like you're holding back." To my relief, this elicited a hearty round of laughter, though I detected more cynicism in it than affection.

Unbelievably, Dick jumped in to save me. I think. "Listen, guys. Someone from Kendrick and Black has to be responsible for us and connect us into their management structure. It isn't like they were just going to leave us alone and have us send smoke signals over the coastal range every quarter letting them know how we're doing."

A few heads nodded to acknowledge the wisdom of his answer.

Amy spoke up, "And it's not like the three of us are going away. Jack isn't going to be here every day. We'll still be handling the day-to-day operations."

I couldn't decide if she was helping me or trying to put me in my place. I let it go, not wanting to come across as defensive. But I couldn't resist exerting my authority a little.

"Right. I'm still responsible for my own client portfolio and for heading up sales for the rest of the strategy practice at K&B. So I'm on the road plenty, and I'm depending on you," I looked to the part of the room where Dick, Amy, and Matt were standing, "to hold down the fort."

That sounded patronizing, and I knew it. Fine. "But you're going to have to be open to some change. Whether that has to do with sales, consulting fees, salary structures, I don't know. But as you all know, when executives say they plan to make no changes to the company they've acquired, they're lying."

Amy spoke next. "Jack, can you tell us a little bit about how K&B is organized, and how it's changed over the years?"

I was glad to move the conversation into less troubled waters, so I spent the next twenty minutes providing an overview of my firm, and generically answering a few innocuous questions about trends in the industry and company benefits. People seemed to lay their torches and pitchforks

35

down for the time being, though I was sure they kept them within reach.

I was feeling like I was going to get out of there relatively unscathed and with no further damage, until someone asked about the culture of the company. "I hear that Kendrick and Black is a sweatshop, and that there is little work-life balance."

The fact that it wasn't really a question, but more a statement, made me feel slightly defensive. I made a bad decision. "Well, I don't know about that. But I will tell you that there are people in our office after six o'clock at night, and if you were to show up on a Saturday you wouldn't be the only one there. I'd say we have a culture of accountability and dedication to clients, and that it's not a great place for someone who prefers a country club," and, as if I hadn't already done enough damage, I continued, "or a playground."

I was sure that the pitchforks and torches were going to start flying, but instead, there was just an extremely awkward silence, followed by Dick bringing the session to an abrupt close.

"Okay, everyone, if there aren't any more questions." He paused for less than a second before continuing. "Thanks for your time. We'll be keeping you posted."

And with that they filed out of the room, a few of them stopping by to shake hands with me, but without any real commentary.

I thought that maybe I had survived the worst of it. I was wrong.

BACKLASH

As soon as the room emptied, I was approached by my three new best friends.

Amy dove in. "Okay. I think we need to spend some time together, and soon, figuring out how this is going to work."

At that point I was really wishing that Marty had come with me, and I was starting to feel like he had simply chickened out. Or maybe I wanted to chicken out myself. Whatever the case, I needed some time to regroup.

I tried to be calm and unruffled. "Yeah, and we're going to need more than a few hours." I paused and looked at my watch. "Unfortunately, I've got to be back in the city in an hour, and I'm out of town the rest of the week."

Dick frowned and was about to say something, so I made my unpopular pitch. "Why don't we get together on Saturday in my office and hammer all this out?"

I hadn't really asked a question as much as made a suggestion. And even though I knew they would hate the idea, I wasn't going to back down. *It's time you guys learned that life on the playground is about to change*, I thought to myself, unsuccessfully fighting off pride and insecurity.

"How about eleven o'clock?"

To their credit, none of them let me see whatever shock they were feeling. They went to their PDAs to check their schedules.

"I'm coaching a soccer game at nine-thirty, so the earliest I can make it is noon." Matt looked at me in a way that suggested defiance and permission at the same time.

I wasn't about to be completely unreasonable. "Does noon work for you guys?" I looked at Amy and Dick.

They nodded.

"Okay, then. I'll make arrangements for lunch. Let's plan on being there until four o'clock or so."

They entered the appointment into their devices as I gathered my things to go.

Then Matt looked at me. "Are you always such an ass, or is this going to get better?"

Well, he didn't actually say that, but I know that's what he was thinking.

I thanked them for their time and showed myself to the door. As I drove away, I decided that the schoolhouse that they called an office was childish, after all, and that these people needed some adult supervision.

And I had a feeling that Saturday was going to be interesting.

DEBRIEF

On the way back to the office I left a message for Marty. By the time I returned, he was sitting at my desk, waiting for me. He didn't bother to get up.

"So, tell me about it. Was it fun?" He grinned like a high school kid questioning a friend about a recent date.

I took my time, milking the drama. "Well, fun isn't exactly the word I would use."

"Okay, what word would you use?"

"Strange. Painful. Those would probably work."

Marty's interest only grew. "Why? What happened?"

And so I began to explain my brief visit to the playground, which was how we started referring to Lighthouse. Marty was riveted, and I have to admit that I probably exaggerated and embellished a little, trying to play to him.

Then I mentioned that we had lost the Boxcar deal to Lighthouse. Marty was stunned.

"You were there just last week. I thought we had the thing closed."

I shrugged. "It gets worse. They said they almost didn't take the gig because they're so busy. A bunch of people are on vacation or something."

Marty shook his head, and I could almost feel his blood pressure rising.

The last thing I wanted to do was make him any angrier, but I knew that I had to show him the binder. He took it from me before I could finish explaining what it was. As he flipped through it, I considered whether I should point out the fee structure or just let him discover it on his own. It didn't take him long.

"Well, this can't be right," he said confidently. "Did you see this page on revenue and fees?"

I nodded. "Actually, it's a little higher. And their clients don't seem to mind."

"Bullcrap," he declared, continuing his perusal of the binder. "I know what we quoted Boxcar, and there is no way they're paying anything close to these rates." Marty paused. "Call them."

"Who? Boxcar?"

"No. Call someone over at Lighthouse and ask them what they're charging."

I hesitated. "You're not serious."

"Of course I'm serious. I want to know."

"Don't you think that will look a little desperate? Or pathetic? Especially so soon after my—"

He cut me off. "I don't care. Listen, we bought them. We own them. They work for us. I don't care what they think."

I wasn't convinced, so he said, "Here, I'll call them myself."

"No, no. That would be even weirder. I'll do it."

Ten minutes later I had my answer. Boxcar was going to pay Lighthouse 10 percent more than we had quoted them! Marty was livid.

"This makes no sense." He looked out the window. "I'm coming to your next meeting with those guys. When is it?"

"Saturday."

"Saturday? Why?"

"For one, I'm on the road the rest of this week." I decided to confess. "And to be honest, I wanted to make a statement about how their work lives are going to be changing."

Marty frowned. "I'm going to the Cal game on Saturday. Let's do it tomorrow instead."

"Tomorrow? Isn't that a little soon?"

Marty shook his head. "Not for me. I'm open after one. We can clear out the rest of the day and go through dinner if we have to. Jim will be here too, so he can stop by and meet his new employees. Do whatever you have to do to rearrange your schedule."

"I'm supposed to be in Dallas tomorrow."

"For the Rockridge meeting? Forget about it. You don't need to be there. This is more important."

The thought of having to back out of that meeting on such short notice wasn't a pleasant one for me. And I didn't like the idea of having Jim Kendrick involved, not this early in a process that was already off to a predictably rocky start. But I could see that Marty was bent on doing this, and I knew him well enough to know that he would get his way.

MESSINESS

Explaining our request for a meeting was not as difficult as I had feared, probably because I didn't present it to Dick as though they had a choice. He agreed to move his and his colleagues' schedules around to accommodate us, which I'm sure was not easy.

I did compromise just a little, agreeing to start at two o'clock so that Matt could make it back from a morning session with a client. Luckily, that client was located in San Francisco, which would cut down his travel time to our office.

Our office was in the Transamerica building—the pointy one that pretty much defines the skyline of San Francisco. Unlike Lighthouse's headquarters, ours was built to impress. The main conference room where we would be meeting was on the twentieth floor and provided a view of Alcatraz, Angel, and Treasure islands, with plenty of bay shipping and sailing traffic to keep the scene moving. The lobby wasn't Old World, but had a sleeker, slightly minimalist feel, a combination of stainless steel, black leather, and mahogany accents.

Though we didn't always wear suits to work, more often than not we wore a tie and a sport coat. Our friends from Half Moon Bay were more of a khaki and loafer crowd.

By one forty-five, Dick, Amy, and Matt had arrived and were waiting in the lobby. They certainly hadn't dressed up for the occasion. I felt much more confident greeting them in my territory, and I decided I would try to make them comfortable.

"Hi everybody. You're early. Traffic must not have been too bad."

Matt explained that his client event didn't go as long as he had anticipated, and his co-workers said their trip was a breeze. They didn't seem to be holding any obvious grudges from our interaction the previous day. I tried to be gracious.

"I'm glad we could do this today instead of Saturday. Whenever we can avoid working a weekend that's a good thing."

They politely agreed, and I brought them into the conference room.

As all visitors did, they marveled at the view, and each of them seemed to have a story about a field trip to Alcatraz or a sailing adventure on the Bay. Amy pointed to Coit Tower at the top of Telegraph Hill and explained that her husband had proposed to her there fourteen years ago.

While we were still gawking and talking, Marty arrived.

He greeted our guests graciously, asking some of the same questions and making some of the same comments about the commute and the view and his relief at not having to do our meeting on Saturday. That was a little embarrassing.

And then we sat down and got started.

SHOW

I kicked off the meeting by setting the context. As it would eventually turn out, I was focused on the wrong areas.

"Okay, I think the most important thing we can do today is go through each of our methodologies. What models and tools we use with our clients. How we evaluate our success with them. How we break out our fees."

Marty jumped in. "As you guys know, there are as many different approaches to consulting as there are consulting firms in the world, and I'm guessing that what we do is pretty different."

"What is that based on?" Matt asked, but not in a defensive way.

"Excuse me?" Marty was suddenly either confused or slightly pissed off.

"I mean, what makes you think that our services and our methodologies are different from yours?"

Marty hesitated. "Well, for one, the size of your firm would indicate that you might do less research than ours. And the mix of consultants you have, in terms of experience, would suggest that you have a less ... " He hesitated. "A less rigorous model in terms of data analysis."

Amazingly, none of the Lighthouse folks flinched. Although they certainly didn't nod their heads in unison to corroborate what Marty had said, they didn't seem at all put off by the presumptuous remark. After a few awkward moments of silence, Dick spoke.

"Why don't we get started? I'm excited to see how all of it compares." He seemed just a little too polite, and I couldn't decide whether I should feel like I was being condescended to.

He continued. "Why don't you guys go first?"

I agreed, opened up my laptop, connected it to the projector on the table, and started my presentation.

For the next ninety minutes, I took them through our entire catalog of tools and models and methodologies. They had plenty of questions—genuine ones, it seemed to me—and Marty and I fielded them with confidence and self-assurance. After we were done, Marty suggested we take a fifteen-minute break, and I showed our guests where the bathrooms and kitchen were, and how to log onto our wireless network to check e-mail.

Marty and I regrouped in his office.

As soon as the door was closed, he started in. "What do you think?"

"About what?"

"I don't know. What do you think they're thinking? Is that Matt guy cocky or what?"

I wasn't sure I agreed with Marty's assessment, but I certainly wasn't going to play devil's advocate with my boss. "I think it's going fine. They seemed to be taking lots of notes, and I think they probably learned some things. Not that they're necessarily unsophisticated, but I'm guessing their tools are a little less up-to-date than ours."

He was waiting for me to go on, so I did.

"I think they're probably a little overwhelmed, wondering what we're thinking."

"What about Matt? What's his deal?"

"He's just insecure. And probably for good reason. He's pretty young."

At that moment the phone rang. Marty looked to see who it was. "That's Kendrick." He picked it up.

After no more than seven seconds of conversation, he hung up and announced with an almost sinister smile on his face, "Jim will be joining us for the next half hour or so. This will be interesting."

We left, for round two.

TELL

When we returned to the conference room, a few minutes later than we had planned, it was empty.

"You think they left?" I joked to Marty, slightly under my breath.

He laughed sheepishly. "Maybe they just decided 'To hell with it.'"

At that moment Amy and Matt came in, followed by Dick, who was carrying a flip chart.

Before we could ask, Amy explained, "Joanne at the front desk found this for us."

Dick set up the easel at the front of the room, and we took our seats.

"Okay, this shouldn't take long," he announced. "Our methodologies are pretty similar to yours."

That was not what I wanted to hear, but I didn't believe him; I decided that I'd be the judge of whether he was right.

Before he could begin, however, Jim Kendrick came into the room.

"Excuse me, everyone. I don't mean to interrupt, but I thought I should come by and say hello."

I stood and introduced my boss's boss to the visitors. They took turns shaking hands while Jim explained that he was the company's namesake and managing partner.

When the formalities were over, Jim dove right in. "I'm sorry for interrupting, but I'd like to ask a few questions and then let you get back to your work." He didn't wait for anyone to acknowledge or accept his apology, but continued. "Can you all give me a quick overview of your backgrounds? As you know, Michael Casey and I did this deal in record time. I'm sure I've glanced at your resumes, but I have to admit that I remember very little detail about you personally. You'll have to forgive me for that." Again, it wasn't really an apology, but rather an explanation. Still, I thought he was being remarkably gracious, at least for him.

Dick went first. "I'll start. I helped Michael start the firm, so I've been with Lighthouse almost fifteen years. I went to Chico State and studied agricultural engineering, and after figuring out that I was tired of the smell of manure, I got a job selling insurance."

Everyone laughed politely.

"Then I was hired by a friend to be a line manager at an automobile manufacturing plant here in the Bay Area, where I worked my way slowly up the ladder. We had a parade of management consultants come through the factory, and I got to know one of them pretty well, and when they offered me a job, I took it. Five years later I met Michael, and two years after that we decided to start doing executive recruiting and coaching."

How old are you? Ninety-five? I wanted to ask.

Jim seemed mildly interested in Dick's story, but it was Marty who was particularly enthralled. He asked the first question.

"How did you guys decide to become a management consulting firm?"

Dick continued, "Well, right away we realized that our clients needed basic strategic help more than anything else, so we started doing that for them. Then they started referring us to other execs who needed help, and before we knew what was happening, we had a growing strategy practice. So we ditched the executive recruiting, moved out to Half Moon Bay, and started what is now Lighthouse."

"Why did you name it Lighthouse?" Jim wanted to know.

For some reason, I decided to explain. "There's a great little lighthouse not far from their office near the coast."

None of my three best friends seemed to mind that I answered for them.

Jim turned to Amy. "How about you?"

She explained that she had attended Fresno State University in the central valley of California where she grew up on an almond farm. She studied business, moved to the Bay Area to be a management trainee at a retail store, then took a line position doing marketing and public relations at a technology company and worked her way up the ladder before joining Lighthouse as a junior consultant.

"And two years ago Michael and Dick forced me to become a partner." She laughed.

"Forced you?" Marty didn't understand.

Dick said, "Yeah. She said she wasn't ready."

"They told me they'd fire me if I didn't do it," she half-joked.

This was all just a little too cute for me, so I moved the conversation along.

"What about you, Matt? What's your story?" I tried to sound friendly, but I wasn't sure it came out that way.

"Well, I'm a little younger than these geezers." We all laughed. "I've been with the company for four years."

He just stopped his bio there, so I decided to become the lead interrogator.

"What did you do before that?"

He looked at Dick and Amy with a smile and seemed slightly nervous. "Well, I worked at my grandfather's bakery."

Again he stopped, and again I pressed him. "And where did you go to school?"

Without hesitating, he replied, "Notre Dame."

Dick and Amy laughed.

"Why is that funny?" Marty wanted to know.

Matt explained, "Because the Notre Dame I went to is actually Notre Dame des Victoires, which is a little Catholic high school in downtown San Francisco." He paused. "I didn't go to college."

Jim was now staring at Matt as though he had just claimed to be an amphibian.

Marty was playing it cool. "So, how did you come to join Lighthouse, Matt?"

Amy jumped in to rescue her younger colleague. "Matt's being a little modest here. The bakery he's referring to is Fanucchi's."

Everyone in the Bay Area knew about Fanucchi's. Their delivery trucks were everywhere, and you could find their products in any grocery store or restaurant within a hundred miles of the Golden Gate Bridge.

Amy continued, "That's a two-hundred-million-dollar company. And Matt wasn't just working there, he was in charge of operations. At age twenty-four."

Dick explained the rest. "We were consulting to Matt's dad, the CEO, and spending a lot of time with Matt and the rest of the management team. A few years later they sold the company to General Mills, and Matt became available."

"Why did you want to be a management consultant?" I asked Matt.

"He didn't," Amy explained. "We recruited him."

Matt added, "Which was hard, because I wanted to go to college. But I was approaching thirty and had two kids."

Dick smiled. "We made him an offer he couldn't refuse."

They laughed.

We didn't.

Dick explained, "This kid had read more business books and case studies than ten Harvard MBAs combined. He paused and looked at me. "No offense, Jack."

I waved it off like it was no big deal, but the worst little part of me wanted to punch him in the face.

Jim Kendrick then said what we were all thinking. "Well, I have to admit that I'm a little surprised by your lack of education and formal training. Which I guess is my own fault because I pulled the trigger on this deal without the benefit of doing any real research."

Any warmth in the room seemed to suddenly disappear.

Marty piled on gently. "I'm curious. Is there anyone at your shop who has a graduate degree?"

Dick nodded. "A couple of them have MBAs."

Matt smiled. "And Christa has a master's from UCLA."

"Who's Christa?" Marty wanted to know.

"Our receptionist," said Amy. "She studied classical literature and is an aspiring screenwriter."

True to form, Jim ended his appearance as abruptly as he started it. "Well, the next few months are going to be interesting, folks." He smiled at his guests, shot Marty and me a raised-eyebrow look that said *What did you get us into?* and left the room.

RECOVERY

We sat in the awkwardness of the moment for a long ten seconds. Jim's departures were always uncomfortable.

Finally, it was Amy who spoke. "Dick, why don't you go ahead and take them through our stuff?"

Marty nodded his agreement, so Dick went to the flip chart, where he spent the next hour summarizing the various tools that he and his colleagues used to help their clients.

I should have taken notes, because a few of the tools he presented were actually interesting and a little different from ours. But I didn't want to give him the satisfaction of thinking I was learning anything new.

By and large, though, the Lighthouse methodology was indeed very similar to what we had been using at K&B as long as I had been there. I found this immensely frustrating. So did Marty, and he did a poor job of hiding it.

"That's it?" he asked, trying his best not to sound critical or judgmental.

Matt reacted. "It's not much different from what you guys presented. Were you expecting more?"

Marty searched for an answer.

Before he could come up with one, Amy offered, "We could certainly go into more detail, if you really want us to. And there are a few other things we've used on occasion. But I was thinking you were more interested in an overview."

Now Marty was ready to respond, and I could tell he really tried to be nice. "No, no, you don't need to go into more detail. Your overview was right on. It's just I thought your approach would be, I don't know, more comprehensive or something."

I decided to change the line of questioning, in search of a major point of differentiation between our firms. "Can you guys tell us how much time your consultants spend at a client? I realize it probably varies, but what's a fairly typical situation?"

Dick raised his eyebrows and looked at his colleagues, as if to say *I haven't really thought of it that way before.*

"Let's see." He looked out the window. "Like you said, it varies from client to client. But if I had to guess, I'd say we're on site with our clients on average ..." He hesitated. "Maybe four or five days a month."

Amy and Matt nodded their agreement.

"Wow." Marty was mildly shocked.

"Does that sound like a lot or a little?" Amy asked.

"A lot! What in the world are you doing there?" Marty was genuinely curious.

"We're working," Matt explained, without the slightest hint of sarcasm.

"And how many clients do you usually work with at any one time?"

54

"You mean the firm, or individual consultants?" Amy asked.

"Individual consultants."

"Most of us have three or four at a time." she said.

Now Marty frowned, like he was trying to solve a puzzle, or a crime.

"You have three or four clients at a time and you spend as much as five days a month with them?"

They nodded, and Marty seemed to be on the verge of asking his big question, when all of a sudden he did an impression of Jim Kendrick by bringing the meeting to an abrupt end.

Taking a deep breath, he announced, "Okay, then. Thanks for rearranging your schedules for us today. This has been really helpful. I feel a lot better about moving forward. I want to get you guys out of here and on the road before traffic gets too bad."

The three visitors seemed as stunned as I was, but went with the plan to avoid any weirdness. Ten minutes later they were gone, and Marty and I were back in the conference room debriefing.

"This just doesn't make any sense," he said.

"Then why did you close down the conversation so fast?"

"Because in situations like this, the only way to figure out what's going on is to see for yourself. It's no different from some of our clients. You can sit around and talk about it all you want, but sometimes you just have to walk the factory floor."

I wasn't sure what he meant. "So what did you have in mind?"

"I think you need to spend most of your time in Half Moon Bay and at their client sites for the next few months. Something doesn't make sense, and we need to understand it."

"But I can't afford to be down there all the time. I've got—"

Marty interrupted me. "Who's the new client you just took on?" he asked.

"You mean Cymerc?"

"Yeah. Forget about them. They're my client now. And hand off the SkyWest project team to Craig. I'll run sales for a few months. That'll allow you to dedicate pretty much all of your time to your Lighthouse team." Something occurred to him and he smiled. "Hey, maybe you can work with Boxcar after all."

The look on my face must have betrayed my dread at what the coming months had in store for me, because before I could say anything, Marty stopped me. "I know this sucks for you. Just make this work, so Kendrick doesn't think we're total idiots. I'm ten months from retirement, and this is the last thing I need."

I felt like I was going to be sick. I had no idea how the next few months would change my life.

ANTICIPATION

The next day was a push as I prepared for my temporary move to Half Moon Bay. From a transportation standpoint it would be a wash, as I lived near the San Francisco Airport and would be doing a reverse commute. But in every other way I braced for what I was sure would be a major transition.

Amy arranged for me to have a desk and phone line installed in Half Moon Bay, and she sent me more information about their clients so I would arrive on Monday morning well-informed.

As I sat on the couch in my family room on Saturday afternoon digesting as much as I could, my wife, Diane, started asking all the right questions.

"Tell me again why you guys bought this company." Diane knew how unenthusiastic I was about my new assignment, and she wanted to help.

"I don't know. It was definitely Marty's thing more than anyone's. And it was more about pride and morbid curiosity than strategy."

"That's ironic, given what you guys do."

I couldn't argue with that. "Consulting firms do a lot of things that would be considered ironic. Or hypocritical. Ego is usually at the heart of it."

"What about you?" she asked.

"What do you mean?"

"Where's your ego in this?"

I put my papers down. "I don't know. I'm pretty sure I've been more of an idiot in the last few days than I have been in a long time. But I just don't like these people. I don't like competing with them. I don't want to be friends with them. I just wish Marty had never convinced Kendrick to do this deal so I wouldn't have to worry about any of it."

"What is it you don't like about them?"

"I don't know. They're just—"

Diane interrupted, "You know, I don't think I've ever heard you say 'I don't know' so many times in one conversation."

I shook my head. "Yeah, it's all confusing to me. I just find them to be a little too casual and oblivious and easygoing. And I can't stand the thought of that firm standing in the way of me taking over the strategy practice."

"How can they stand in the way?"

"Well, if this integration doesn't go well, and if we can't figure out why their financials look better than ours, Jim Kendrick certainly isn't going to be feeling great about giving 27 percent of the firm's revenue to me. All of a sudden my career seems to be riding on my ability to deal with a bunch of people who look like they should be working at the Gap."

She smiled in a warm and motherly way. "I think you need to leave your ego behind when you go out there on Monday."

"Yeah, yeah," I said as I dove back into my reading. I knew Diane was right, but I also knew I was nowhere near the point of being able to do what she suggested.

REENTRY

As I made my second drive on the two-lane highway to the coast, I had a sudden eerie feeling that I might never make it back to my office at K&B in San Francisco. Dismissing it as paranoia, I drove westward.

When I caught my first glimpse of the blue-striped cylinder marking my approach to my new office, I decided that I didn't like lighthouses after all. Wishing I could bring Diane with me to work, I pulled myself out of my Lexus and went inside.

"*Surprise!*" The entire office was there shouting to me, and Dick was holding a big cake with the words "Welcome to our company, Jack Bauer!" stenciled in blue icing across the chocolate top. They lifted me onto their shoulders and began singing "For He's a Jolly Good Fellow."

Of course that's not what happened. In fact, there was no one sitting at the front desk. It was eight-fifteen in the morning and barely anyone was there. I did find an envelope on the front desk with the name "Jack" written neatly across the front. Inside was a note from Amy, in which she indicated where my desk was and that we would have a meeting at nine-thirty. She did write "Welcome" at the bottom, which was a far cry from a cake, but nice to see, I had to admit.

My desk was in the building across the quad from the reception area, in the same part of the office that the three partners shared. Getting used to sitting in the open, without privacy, was going to be an adjustment for me. But then again, ~~so was going pee-pee in a urinal built for a fifth-grader.~~

By the time our nine-thirty meeting rolled around, I was glad for something real to do.

This was our weekly executive committee meeting, and once again, I found myself sitting alone with my three new BFFs.

"How was the commute, Jack?" Matt seemed genuinely interested, even warm.

"Twenty-eight minutes door to door," I reported. "Not bad. That's actually ten minutes faster than my ride to the city."

We made small talk for a few minutes until Dick kicked things off.

"Okay, what we usually do at these meetings is talk about what we've got on our plates for the week, how we're doing in terms of our primary goals for the period, and then take on one or two key issues that might be fixable in the near term."

I nodded.

"But today, we thought we'd give you a chance to ask us any questions you might have." He paused and changed his tone just slightly. "And ask you a few of our own."

I responded without thinking much. "Why don't you go first? I'm guessing you've given some thought to the questions you have for me."

Dick smiled, looked at his colleagues, and took a breath. "Okay, here's the deal, Jack. We're going to have to work together, at least for a while, and so we might as well be

61

honest with each other. We're a little confused about some things, and we'd appreciate it if you told us where you're coming from."

Taking a deep breath myself, I tried to think about Diane's advice. "Fire away."

Amy began, "Okay, I have a question, and I don't want you to think I'm attacking you."

"That usually means an attack is coming," I smiled.

Amy was quick to explain, "No, no. That's not what I meant."

"It's okay. I was joking. Go ahead."

A little calmer now, she continued. "Alright, I'd like to know why you haven't asked us a single question about Michael Casey."

Suddenly I felt myself blushing, and I was sure they noticed. I tried to be cool. "Well, I don't know." There was that phrase again. "I guess I just assumed that if there was something you wanted me to know ..." I paused, which gave Dick a chance to interrupt.

He wasn't buying it for a second. "There is a lot you need to know about him."

I braced myself for a lecture, but it didn't come.

Mercifully, he went on, "But that will come in time as you learn more about the company. First we want to make sure that you get to know our clients, what's going on with us right now, that kind of stuff."

Doing my best to take my wife's advice, I rose above my own pride and pettiness. "Well, I'll admit that I'd like to know more about why Michael decided to sell the business. It still doesn't make sense to me."

Amy took this one. "Obviously you know why he left in the first place." It was a question more than a statement.

I shook my head.

Dick was incredulous. "You mean they didn't tell you? What *did* they tell you?"

"Just that it was for personal reasons. Wanting to spend more time with his family or something."

"But that can mean anything. It's usually code for 'He screwed up big time,'" said Matt.

I agreed. "Yeah, I figured it was something like that."

Everyone paused, amazed at what I didn't know.

"So, is anyone going to tell me the truth?"

Dick nodded his head, but he wasn't happy. "Sure. I just can't believe no one told you any of this. What kind of firm do you work for?" He paused. "I'm sorry, it's just a little bizarre to me. Anyway, Michael has three grown kids, and his oldest daughter lives in Texas with her family, two young girls."

He paused again, and I waited patiently for him to continue.

"Six weeks ago she and her husband were sideswiped by a semi truck. Her husband died, and she sustained very serious injuries."

"What about the kids?" I wanted to know.

"They were at home."

I was relieved, but only for as long as it took to realize the situation those kids were now in.

Amy picked up the story. "Michael and Liz, his wife, went there immediately. She hasn't been back since. Michael's just come back to wrap up the sale of the company. He's now in San Antonio taking care of his daughter and her children."

It took a few moments for me to recalibrate what had been in my head for the past week and to digest the situation. And then something hit me.

"I'm guessing you know his daughter pretty well, being that this is such a small company."

Amy nodded. "We went to her wedding. My daughters were her flower girls. Dick's the godfather to one of her daughters. We all went to the funeral."

It wasn't like anyone in the room was about to cry; they had certainly already begun the process of dealing with this. But I was surprised at how much it affected me. I thought of my own kids, and the fact that I had never even met Marty's children.

After a few moments to digest this, I came up with a question, which I asked delicately. "So, why did he sell the company? Why didn't he just let you guys run it, or sell it to you?"

Dick smiled at his colleagues in a way that said, *There's that question again.*

"Selling it to Kendrick was the right thing to do," he explained.

"Why?"

"Well," Matt said, "for one, Michael's never coming back. His daughter's injuries are serious ones, and he was adamant that taking care of her family was his new full-time job."

Damn it. I had to respect Michael Casey. I had really hoped that I could keep loathing him.

Matt went on. "Selling it to us would have put a huge, risky burden on us. If Michael's departure hurt the business, the value of the firm could have disappeared. Michael wanted us to share in some financial upside, and this was the right time to do it."

"Besides," Amy explained, "if things don't work out with K&B, we can always take a year off and go start another firm."

I couldn't argue with the logic I was hearing. "So why do you think K&B did the deal?" I wanted to get their perspective.

"You want our honest answer?" Amy asked.

I opened my eyes wide and nodded my head as if to say I can't wait to find out.

"Well, we think that you—not you personally, but someone over there—didn't like us and wanted to get rid of us. Not like the mafia or anything."

We laughed.

"But it sure didn't feel like a marriage made in heaven."

"And then there's the deep pockets." Matt explained. "Kendrick and Black can afford to take a flyer on us, but that's a lot of money to our little firm. We received a nice little payout, and we get to keep our jobs."

I didn't want to tell them that there was a good chance some of them wouldn't. As it turns out, I didn't have to.

"And if some people don't get to keep their jobs," Dick explained, "then they'd get a severance package to add to their payout, which would be more than enough to bridge them through to their next job."

It was at that moment that I was about to embrace these people—not literally, of course—and become part of the team. But then it dawned on me. They were actually in a better position than I was! If things didn't go well with the merger, they'd be fine. Probably better off. But my career would be in serious trouble.

The more I learned about Lighthouse Partners, the worse I felt about myself and about the state of my career. And that put me in a horrible situation. I had to make this merger work with a bunch of people who constantly reminded me that I was sometimes a complete ass.

Fortunately, my wife was a much better person than I was.

ADVICE

That night I put my kids to bed early—with more affection than I had in a long time—and helped Diane clean the kitchen more than I usually do. My motives were not pure. I needed her advice.

Sitting down in the kitchen, I explained my predicament.

"So I'm stuck with these people for at least a few months, I'm guessing. I don't particularly like them, which might not be fair, but it is what it is. And if I can't salvage this thing, Marty is going to look bad and throw me under the bus when he retires."

Diane listened patiently.

"This is all Marty's mess, and he's making me deal with it. It isn't fair," I complained.

"You're right. It isn't fair." Diane was neither patronizing nor cold. "But it wasn't fair that those kids lost their dad, and that their mom can't care for them, either."

"I know that. I realize that I seem like a selfish jerk right now. But that doesn't change the fact that I'm being asked to do something that isn't possible."

"Why do you think it isn't possible?"

"Because Kendrick thinks they're a bunch of yahoos from the beach. Marty can't stand them. I'm supposed to make the

67

deal work, but in a way that allows Marty and Jim to keep hating them. And now I realize that these people would probably be better off if the whole thing blew up. Heck, a year from now Marty will be retired, these Lighthouse people will be sitting at home counting their severance packages, and I'll be looking for a job and trying to explain why I flamed out at one of the most prestigious consulting firms in the country."

Diane smiled at me.

"Oh, I hate when you do that."

"What?" she asked.

"Give me that smile that says you know what I should do."

She laughed. "I think you know what I think you should do."

I shook my head. "I got nothing."

"Come on. You should go in there and learn everything you can about that little firm, and make this the best acquisition that Jim Kendrick has ever done."

Before I could say anything, she went on, "And who cares if Marty gets the credit? You'll still get promoted, and you'll be better for the experience."

I shook my head again—not to disagree, but because I knew she was right and that I was going to have to become a better person to make this work.

"I hate personal growth."

Diane laughed and gave me a hug. I thought about Michael Casey's daughter.

PART THREE

Research

EXPOSURE THERAPY

The next day was the beginning of my personal crash course in Lighthouse Partners and Michael Casey, the man.

During my first three days in Half Moon Bay I met with at least a dozen consultants and most of the other staff members. I sat in on a handful of account reviews, analyzed the financials of the firm in greater depth, and went through a personality profile called the Myers-Briggs with Amy. (I turned out to be an ENTP, whatever that means.)

And in spite of the fact that the people at Lighthouse were friendly, if not a little too casual for my taste, I learned nothing that helped me understand why the firm had been successful and how we were going to extract any goodness from them.

It wasn't until my fourth day that I saw my first glimpse of the secret behind the success of this strange little firm.

Dick asked me to go on a sales call with him, and I gladly agreed, wanting to get out of the office. On the way, he explained that we were going to stop by one of his clients, a fast-growing regional chain of upscale Mexican restaurants called Mariscos. Dick had canceled a meeting with the head of marketing there the week before in order to meet with us in the city, and he wanted to check in on a new branding initiative they had been working on. He also thought it would be a good opportunity for me to meet one of the firm's older clients, even if it was one of the smallest.

The restaurant chain's headquarters wasn't what I expected. I guess I had hoped it would be an adobe structure next to a mission, complete with a guy out front taking a nap under a big sombrero. But it was just a plain, glass-walled building with an unattractive lobby and a receptionist named Marge. Marge wasn't necessarily unattractive. Just the lobby.

Dick knew her by name, and I was a little surprised that Marge didn't flinch when he walked by her and into the office area behind the reception desk without getting a badge or needing an escort. We passed by a series of offices and cubicles decorated with food advertisements and other Mexican paraphernalia. More than a few of the cube dwellers greeted Dick.

Eventually we reached a windowed office where the door was closed. Through the floor-to-ceiling window in the hallway we could see a guy in a sport coat sitting behind a desk talking on the phone. He waved us in, but kept talking into his handset.

"No, we can't do that until we've opened up the Boston and Toronto stores."

He pointed to the chairs in front of his desk to provoke us to sit down.

"No, Montreal can wait. Listen, Tim. I've got some visitors here, so I have to go. I'll talk to you on Wednesday. Bye."

As soon as he hung up the phone, the man I would later learn was the head of marketing at Mariscos stood up and extended his hand to me. "You must be the new guy. Hi, I'm Charlie."

I shook his hand and told him my name.

"So, you're the guy who's going to make something of this hopeless little consulting firm, huh?"

He and Dick laughed. I think I did too.

I tried to be nice. "I don't think they need any help from me."

Charlie changed the subject, teasing his consultant. "So, Dick, you blew me off last week. Had to go to the city to meet with the big boys."

Dick held up his hands. "It wouldn't have been a good start to refuse my first meeting with Jim Kendrick."

Charlie suddenly had an idea. "Hey, come with me." Before I knew what was happening, he was out from behind his desk and through the door in his office.

We followed him to a conference room where a half dozen easels had been set up around a big table. Each held a poster depicting artists' renditions of a storefront, a logo, a website, even a business card. Each poster had a green and red border around a silhouetted picture of a fisherman in a boat.

"So, these are the mock-ups the creative people sent us on Friday. We've got to decide by the end of the month. What do you think?" Charlie was obviously excited.

Dick looked at them for a few seconds, frowning. "I'm sorry," he began, "but I don't think these are right."

At first Charlie looked like he thought Dick was kidding. "Really?"

Dick nodded. "Yeah. I mean, I thought you decided you wanted to move away from the refried beans and piñata scene. Create more of a Latin feel."

"We do," Charlie countered. "We want to differentiate from all the tired and typical Mexican restaurants."

"Well, it looks pretty typical to me. I mean, all you need is to put a picture of a guy in a big hat taking a nap, and you've got it perfect."

I almost laughed.

Dick seemed a little harsh, but Charlie laughed too, glanced at the door, and then whispered to Dick. "Mike likes it."

I would later learn that Mike was Miguel Cantos, the owner of the restaurant chain.

Dick didn't hesitate. "Well, bring him in here then. We can't let him do this."

Charlie shook his head and smiled, but in a slightly pained way. "I'll be right back."

As soon as he left, Dick turned to me. "We did a bunch of competitive research for them, even focus groups. And everything said they needed to be attracting a younger, more upscale crowd. And they're planning to expand into the Northeast and Canada, where most of the Hispanics aren't Mexican."

We inspected the posters in silence for a few minutes, until he shook his head again. "This stuff is terrible."

"What's terrible?" The question came from the company's well-dressed CEO, a gray-haired man who was now standing behind us.

Dick didn't hesitate. "These mock-ups. This isn't delivering on what we agreed to a couple of weeks ago, is it?"

"These were done by one of the top agencies in the city. I don't think they're terrible at all. I like them."

"What do you like about them?" Dick asked politely but with confidence.

Mike took a breath. "They're much classier than what we have now. They make it clear that our specialty is fish." He paused. "And we already paid fifteen thousand dollars for them."

We laughed.

Dick didn't let up. "Come on, Mike. We talked about being more like P.F. Chang's and less like Red Lobster. This is pretty Red Lobster."

Mike wasn't smiling now. "I think you're wrong."

"No, you don't," Dick countered, teasing slightly. "You just don't want to tell those creative people that they whiffed on this."

I could not believe what I was hearing. Mike didn't seem to find any humor in Dick's comment, but he didn't seem particularly upset at him either. Even Charlie wasn't at all ruffled by the exchange.

"Listen," Dick continued. "I have no vested interest in one design or another. And I'll be the first to admit that I don't have a creative bone in my body. All I know is that I'm not going to pay nineteen bucks for a Chilean sea bass at a restaurant that looks like that." He pointed at the poster with the storefront on it.

Mike didn't say a word, but continued staring at the poster that Dick had pointed to. Finally, he weighed in. "Neither would I."

Charlie finally spoke up, and as usual made a joke. "I wouldn't pay five dollars for Chilean sea bass."

Mike smiled. "Yeah, but you don't like fish. Let's try this again."

We laughed, and Charlie scolded his consultant. "Now I have to go back and talk to those artsy-fartsy guys again. Thanks a lot, Dick."

Dick was back to business. "Hey, are we still on for the twenty-seventh?"

Mike nodded. "Everyone will be there."

Then Dick finally introduced me to Mike. We exchanged pleasantries until Dick explained that we were on our way to an appointment, and we left.

On the way to San Jose for our sales meeting, I didn't know how to act. Technically, I was Dick's boss, but I felt more like his guest. And given that I was fifteen years younger than him, I didn't want to sound critical.

"Are you always so direct with your clients?" (Trust me. It came out sounding nice.)

"Are you kidding? That was nothing. You should have been there when I told Mike I thought he needed to replace his last head of marketing."

"That's a little more typical, though. I'm talking about the way—"

Dick interrupted. "The head of marketing was his son."

I laughed out loud. "Wow. How did he take it?"

"Mike or his son?"

"Both."

"Jimmy, his boy, was actually easier than his dad. He knew he was in over his head, and he wanted to be in operations anyway. Mike moved him into the field, where he's running two of the newest restaurants."

Dick laughed. "Mike was a different story. He did not want to hear that his son was the problem on the management team. And no one else was going to tell him."

"How did you broach that subject with him?"

"Well ... " Dick thought about it. "If I remember correctly, I said, 'Mike, I think Jimmy is the problem on the management team.'"

Again I couldn't help but laugh. "Come on." I didn't believe him.

"I'm serious."

"You must know this guy pretty well to say something like that to him."

Dick agreed. "Yeah, I know him very well. But at the time I didn't. I mean, we had been working with them for a couple of months, but we've become closer since then." He thought about it for a second. "In fact, that's probably when the relationship grew the most."

"So what did he say? Did he argue with you?"

"Well, to be clear, I didn't just go into his office and announce that his son was incompetent. I respected the fact that any dad would have a hard time coming to grips with the idea that a family member needed to be addressed. So I told him about the time that I had to bench one of my boys in baseball for having a bad attitude, and how my wife and my other kids were mad at me. As it turned out, my son didn't like baseball, which was why he was acting out. He started playing tennis instead and wound up getting a partial athletic scholarship in college."

"What would you have done if he had kicked you out of his office?"

"I'd have left his office. But that wasn't going to happen."

"You weren't concerned at all then?" I pushed him.

"Well, it wasn't easy, if that's what you mean. But Michael Casey always said that if we weren't willing to tell a client the kind truth, why should they pay us?"

Though I should have been over it by now, I still wasn't ready to start asking questions about Michael. So I just stored all of this somewhere in the recesses of my brain and changed the subject.

"So, tell me about this potential client we're pitching to today."

GIVE AWAY

"Ram Transport is a trucking company, one of the top ten in the country, I think. We're meeting with the CEO and the head of operations."

"What kind of revenue do they do?"

Dick thought about it. "I'm not sure exactly."

I thought it was odd that he didn't know, but I assumed he just didn't have the exact figure in front of him.

"How many employees?" I asked.

He didn't flinch. "I don't know. I'm not even sure how many of their people are independent contractors or full-time staff. I'm guessing that most of their drivers aren't employees."

I decided that this wouldn't be the best time to challenge Dick's preparation regimen, so I stopped my questions. Soon enough we pulled off the freeway and into the parking lot of an office complex near the San Jose Airport.

As we got out of Dick's Acura, I noticed something strange. The only thing in Dick's hand was a black leather portfolio.

Without thinking, I asked, "Is that all you're bringing?"

Dick looked surprised. "Yeah, why?"

"You're not going to do a presentation? No proposal? Do you have any handouts?"

Dick shook his head. "Nope." He looked at the folder in his hands and smiled. "Heck, this thing is just a prop." He opened up the portfolio to reveal that it held nothing but a pad of paper and a pen. "I'd feel kind of strange if I weren't carrying something."

I was starting to think that our initial assessment of Lighthouse was accurate after all, and that they must be running an illegal narcotics distribution business to make their numbers look so good, maybe taking middle-of-the-night shipments in Half Moon Bay and storing the drugs in that lighthouse. It would have been a good story.

We went into the building, and this time the receptionist didn't just let us roam free, but gave us security badges and had us wait for someone to get us. The lobby was typical corporate, clean and professional, nothing attractive or interesting.

Within minutes we were greeted by a woman who was an administrative assistant of some kind. She escorted us to the elevators and to a conference room, where we declined her offer of coffee or soda and waited for what I thought was going to be a sales presentation.

When the CEO and head of ops arrived, we did our typical meet and greet and sat down to talk. The CEO went first.

"So, I was telling my friend, John Sullivan—he's the COO over at Frigidata—that we needed some help figuring out how to do better planning, and he said I should call you. And that's why we're here."

Dick nodded. "Okay. Tell me why you think you need to do better planning."

The CEO looked to his operating guy. "Well, it's getting harder and harder to make revenue forecasts. Our costs are rising faster than they should be, and we're not sure why. And we're starting to lose market share, which hasn't happened in ten years."

Pulling out his pad of paper, Dick began asking a series of questions. Revenue. Number of employees. Competitive landscape. Cost structure.

I couldn't believe it.

If this were my sales call, I'd have come to the meeting already knowing the answers to these questions. I'd be using industry language and referring to anything I'd read in the *Journal* or in trade reports. Hell, I'd probably be 75-percent sure what we'd propose doing for the client. And here Dick was, doing basic, primary research during his first sales call.

What was worse, the clients didn't seem to mind.

After he had exhausted his initial questions, Dick went to the whiteboard. "Okay, let me explain what a strategically healthy company looks like, and figure out whether any of this is helpful to you."

He drew a diagram similar to one that we used from time to time. Basic. Then he wrote a few questions next to it having to do with customers and competitors and core principles.

And for the next forty-five minutes we just talked. Or better yet, Dick asked questions and the CEO and his sidekick talked. From time to time Dick would draw another diagram

Getting Naked

or chart, almost always the right one given what they were talking about, and the clients would get animated.

At one point the same assistant who had greeted us in the lobby came in to remind them that they had a conference call in ten minutes. They asked her to push it back by an hour. They were too involved in the conversation to stop now.

For another forty five minutes we—yes, even I joined in the session—talked about whether the problem they were facing was really a planning issue or more about clarity around competition. I have to admit that it was fascinating, and the time flew by.

Finally, the CEO looked up at the clock and said, "Okay, we're running out of time here. I'd like to continue this conversation with the rest of my team, because we're going to need input from marketing and finance to figure this out."

Dick nodded. "Okay. Should we shoot for next week?"

The two men who were already acting like clients looked at each other, nodding.

"Why don't we use the second part of our staff meeting on Tuesday for this?" the ops guy asked his boss.

Dick scrolled through his PDA. "I'm good for Tuesday afternoon."

"Done. We'll be in the board room on the fourth floor. I'll have Nancy set you up."

I felt like I was going crazy, or that I was watching a bad movie about business. No one had even mentioned fees or contracts or scopes of engagement. Finally, the CEO restored my faith in humanity.

"So, should we talk about what this is going to cost?"

82

Dick didn't seem surprised, but he certainly wasn't waiting for the question. "If you want, we could, I guess. But why don't I just come next week and we'll see how it goes. If you decide we can help you, we can figure it out from there."

The CEO seemed to like that idea. He eagerly shook our hands, thanked us for our time, and genuinely remarked, "I'm looking forward to next week."

And we were gone.

I was stunned. It reminded me of the time in high school when I finally got up the courage to ask Christine Owens to the prom. "Okay," she said, almost immediately. "Pick me up at seven-thirty."

It was all too easy.

CONSISTENCY

At first, I didn't have the courage—or, perhaps, the humility—to challenge or congratulate or even ask questions of Dick about what he had just done. All I could do was try to convince myself that it was one of those fluky situations where everything comes together at once. *I'm sure every sales pitch doesn't go like that*, I tried to convince myself.

I decided that I couldn't hold it in.

"So, I'm curious," I said, still trying to play it cool. "Why didn't you try to wrap up the deal today? I think they'd have agreed to just about anything." And then, in a rare moment of graciousness, I added, "By the way, you did a great job in there."

"Thanks. Your input was helpful."

He didn't seem like he was going to answer my question, but before I could ask it again, he explained.

"You know, I'm pretty sure they're going to want to be a client. So I don't really want them thinking about what we're trying to get out of the arrangement. At this point, all I want to focus on is figuring out their issues." He paused, and again, just before I could ask a follow-up question, continued: "And we need to make sure that they'd be the right kind of client. We'll have a better sense of that next week."

"What do you mean?" I was confused. "What would make them the wrong kind of client?"

Dick didn't hesitate. "Well, for all I know the real problem is the CEO. If that's the case, and he's not willing to deal with that, then we don't want to be in there wasting our time and energy, and their money, rearranging deck chairs on the Titanic."

I laughed. "I'd be glad to waste their money rearranging the deck chairs, as long as they paid me enough."

Dick laughed too. "We've learned over the years that having a bad client is worse than having none."

"How could that be if they're paying you?"

Dick didn't have to think about it. "Well, for one, it prevents you from finding other good clients. And you're unlikely to get a good reference. In fact, they're likely to tell everyone they know how you weren't able to help them, because they certainly aren't going to admit it was their fault." He paused. "And, as Michael used to say, it just makes you feel bad about coming to work. It destroys the culture."

I didn't say anything. Mostly, I wasn't buying the logic, and maybe even the sincerity, of what he was saying. This was, after all, a business, and revenue is a big part of that.

Without the slightest hint of defensiveness, he asked me a question. "So what would you have done?"

I thought about it. "I don't know. I guess the whole thing would have been different. I'd have gone in there with a bunch of research and a slide presentation. I'd probably show them other work we've done for clients, to give them a sense of our capabilities. I'd have given them a bio of our consulting team and a list of references they could call. And I'd probably tell them what they could expect to pay, too."

And then it dawned on me. I was a salesman. Dick was just a consultant. He didn't do any selling at all. Instead, he just went in there and started helping them.

I had more questions for him. "Do you ever worry that you're going to do too much during your sales call, and that the client will take it and use it and not hire you?"

Dick smiled. "That's exactly what Matt said after his first few sales calls. And no, I don't worry about it. Very few people are going to do something like that. If they need help, they need help. Even if what I show them makes perfect sense, they usually know they need help implementing it and getting the rest of their team on board."

I was surprised that I agreed with him.

"And besides," he went on, "even if they did do that, then they'd probably be a pretty lousy client anyway. So it would be better to find that out up front."

Again, I felt like I was sitting next to Christine Owens on the way to the prom. It was all too easy. If only Dick had been wearing a corsage, the scene would have been perfect.

SPEED READING

Almost every day for the next two weeks I learned something new and strange about Michael Casey and his odd little firm. And I wrote it all down, both because I needed to figure out what was going on, and because it was fascinating. And painful.

Soon enough I realized that they had a fairly long list of principles that Michael had been espousing over the years, but otherwise not much structure around their approach. I'm a structure guy, so naturally I was trying to figure out the unseen model behind it all.

Well, I didn't go with Dick to the follow-up meeting at Ram Transport because Amy and I decided it would be more interesting, and useful, for me to help her with a two-day off-site meeting she was doing for a client in Walnut Creek, a city on the east side of the Bay.

During the morning drive eastward across the San Mateo Bridge, Amy gave me some background about the client. MediTech was a medium-sized software company that helped hospitals, doctors, and insurance companies automate records management and prescription drug tracking. Though they had hired Lighthouse to help them assess the efficacy of a merger they were considering, the work had shifted toward organizational dynamics. This included getting the executive team aligned around a common strategy, and breaking down barriers between departments.

Some people, including me at one point in my career, thought this kind of thing was "touchy-feely." I had come around to believing that it was usually the biggest problem that most clients faced. The key was having a practical approach that yielded results—and that didn't entail any hugging or interpretive dancing.

The first half of the first day of the off-site was focused on the company's strategy, with heavy emphasis on technology. Though I wasn't completely unfamiliar with technical issues, I was usually a little in the dark when it came to anything sophisticated. Combine that with a bunch of new medical terms and more three-letter acronyms than I could possibly remember, and my head was spinning. I figured I was the only one in the room lost in the depth of the conversations.

But on more than one occasion, Amy did something that was at once ridiculous and wonderful. Often, when the chief technology officer or one of the medical doctors on the team started using an acronym or term that I didn't understand, she would interrupt and ask them what it meant. Evidently she didn't know either.

And a few times, the answer was obvious. Once she even provoked a parental smile from the CEO when she asked him a question that you could have known from watching *ER* on TV for one season. But more often than not, when Amy asked a question, one or two of the others in the room turned out to be just as confused as she was.

As simple as this was, I couldn't help but think that I would have been mortified to ask a client those questions. Though I would have been terrified of being caught, I would simply have pretended to know what they were talking about and then looked up the terms during a break or, if I was feeling particularly bold, ask someone quietly, one on one. Amy didn't seem to care what they thought.

And her boldness wasn't limited to questions. She threw out a few suggestions that had me scratching my head. One had to do with patient records, if I remember correctly. Some of the executives were talking about how to make them more easily accessible, and Amy made a suggestion that was greeted with mild if not good-natured surprise. I'm not sure what a guffaw is, but I think I heard a few of those, too.

And I remember someone saying, "But that would be in complete violation of HIPAA!" which has to do with privacy. What amazed me the most about the situation, more than the reaction of the clients, was the way Amy handled it.

She was surprised at first that her suggestion was so off base, but then she seemed to shrug it off almost immediately. And although I expected it to be an uncomfortable moment for her and the rest of the people in the room, I'm sure if you were to ask them about it now, none would remember it. It was that uneventful.

On another occasion, one that probably none of them remember either, Amy made a ridiculous suggestion. It was a conversation about a small competitor in another region of the country that had a much better user interface for their product than MediTech. They were lamenting the difficulty of selling a product that seemed harder to use and wondering how they could imitate their competitor.

"Why don't you just license their technology?" Amy asked. "I bet they'd let you do that."

No one reacted. I was certain they were simply trying to avoid or, at the very least, mitigate the discomfort of the moment so that Amy wouldn't be embarrassed.

Finally, the technology guy said, "You know, I've been wondering about the same thing. It wouldn't hurt them to let us use it, and they'd get some revenue out of it."

The head of business development jumped in. "In my last company, we did the same thing with a company in the U.K. Since our markets were so different, they thought it was a great idea."

And just like that, Amy was off the hot seat—not that she ever looked like she was sitting on it in the first place. And I have to admit, if you asked her about it today, I'm sure she wouldn't remember that one either.

I was starting to wonder—or, to be more accurate, to worry—about how I would explain any of this to Marty. Of course, I had no idea that the second day of the off-site would be even better. And crazier.

DANGER

my and I went to dinner with the MediTech team that evening, so by the next morning I was feeling fairly comfortable with the group. Most were friendly and interesting people, but one woman, in particular, was a little less friendly and a lot more interesting than the others.

Her name was Mikey (or maybe Mickey, but I'll go with Mikey), and she was the head of marketing. There was just something skeptical—or more accurately, cynical—about her. Whenever a problem arose, she made it clear that it wasn't her fault and that if everyone had just listened to her, there would be no problem at all.

At first it was bearable. But after sitting next to her at dinner, it became annoying. And by the second day I wanted to strangle her, though I have to admit that I was a little frightened of someone who could be that cynical and self-confident.

Anyway, it was almost lunchtime on day two, and we were talking about competitors and how we were going to position ourselves against them. She started in on how great the last company she had worked for was, and how we should have adopted a different technology platform years ago than the one MediTech had chosen, and on she went.

By now I had come to realize that the team's way of dealing with her was just to let her rant and then resume their conversation. As uncomfortable as that was, I couldn't think of a better solution.

But then there was Amy. Holding up her hand like she was asking a question of Sister Rose Marie in second grade, she didn't wait to be called on. "I'm sorry, but I think it's time we dealt with something, because I don't think we're going to make this strategy work if we don't."

The room was quiet, though I'm pretty sure they had no idea what Amy was about to do.

"Mikey, I'm sure you mean well." She paused long enough for the room to reach a completely new level of silence, and for Mikey to raise her eyebrows. "But when you approach every issue with such . . . ," she searched for the right word, "negativity, it's a real buzz kill for the team."

(On the way home I learned that Amy didn't know the original meaning of a buzz kill. I was liking her more and more.)

Amy continued, "I mean, are you noticing how the room goes quiet when you do that? And what about the rest of you? Am I the only one?"

The third-grader inside me wanted to stand up and shout, "This is the best off-site ever!"

No one spoke.

"Or maybe it's just me," Amy said, looking a little uncomfortable now.

More silence.

Finally, the CFO, another woman, weighed in. "I have to agree, Mikey. It just seems like you're never happy, and that everything is always someone else's problem."

Amy walked right over to the CEO and stood in front of him, but without looking at him. Somehow, this seemed to provoke him to weigh in.

"Okay, you guys know I hate talking about this kind of stuff. I went to med school, for heaven's sake, and I like dealing with medical stuff."

They laughed a little.

"But we've got to deal with this. And yes, I see it, and I know others in the room do too."

A few heads nodded in a barely perceptible way. The tension was peaking.

Amy stepped right into the middle of it. "Here's the thing. Every team has issues like this, so this isn't something that we can't deal with. And I'm sure that every person in the room has an area where they can improve, and that if they did, the team would be exponentially better off."

No one nodded their heads, but there seemed to be an unspoken agreement in the air.

"So let's take a few minutes," she paused, "no, more like ninety minutes, and deal with this."

A few of the team members, most notably the chief technology officer, sighed in a complaining kind of way. Amy took him on.

"Come on, Jim. Are you telling me that this kind of stuff doesn't make a difference? Do you think we're going to come anywhere close to tapping into the technology that you've put together if we keep wasting time and energy like this?"

He responded. "I know. But do we really need to take an hour and half? I mean, we've got real work to do."

Amy was about to respond, when the CEO stepped in.

"Wait a second, Jim. You know how many times you've come by my office and complained about this."

Everyone seemed to sneak a glance at Mikey to see how she would react. Stone cold.

The CEO went on, with a little more emotion than he looked like he was accustomed to showing. "Frankly, I'm tired of it."

Finally, Mikey stood up. "Okay. Here's the thing." She took a big breath. "I know I'm a pain in the ass. I left the last start-up I worked for because I had a hard time with the executives there."

This was better than TV.

"But that's not going to happen again. So I'd appreciate it if you guys would just tell me straight up when I'm pissing you off, because I can take it." She paused. "What I can't take is you telling each other, or him," she pointed at the CEO, "and me finding out later."

She sat down.

The CEO looked at Amy as if to say *back to you*, and she proceeded to take the group through one of the most intense, interesting, and—from what I saw—effective behavioral therapy exercises I had ever witnessed. All in a little more than an hour.

Starting with the CEO, they went around the room and told him what they thought his most valuable attribute was for the team, and then they went around and told him the one thing they thought he should work on. The answers were pretty consistent; he took them well, and promised to do his best to address his biggest area of weakness, which I don't remember.

Then they went around the table and did the same for everyone else, including Mikey.

At one point she almost cried, but interestingly, it was when they told her that she was one of the most creative marketing people they had ever met. And they meant it. When they explained to her that she was way too defensive and critical of everyone else, she accepted it and reiterated her desire for them to hold her accountable. And as far as I could tell, she meant that too.

When it was over, there was a palpable sense of relief among the team members, even laughter. It was incredible. I thought the team should have lifted Amy onto their shoulders and paraded her around the room. Instead, they went to the bathroom.

DIGESTION

The rest of the session was pretty much a blur for me, as I tried to process what I had been witnessing, not only that day but during my first few weeks at Lighthouse.

The two-hour drive home with Amy gave me a chance to do some debriefing.

"How typical was that session?" I asked, trying not to betray the awe that I had felt.

Amy thought about it. "I don't know if any session is typical. They're all a little different."

"Right. But in terms of the level of tension and drama, how did that one rate?"

She laughed. "Oh, that was definitely on the dramatic side. I don't usually have to do anything like that." She paused. "But stranger things than that have happened more than a few times over the years."

I wasn't about to let her get away with that statement without asking for details, so she told me some seriously unbelievable stories about difficult clients and embarrassing moments. The best one had to do with a time that Michael Casey was giving a strategy presentation to a room full of executives at a big client's worldwide planning meeting.

"The CEO and his executive team worked with Michael for three weeks putting together the content for the meeting, crunching numbers, creating slides, and reviewing the key priorities and messages for what was looking like a particularly difficult year." Amy shook her head in disbelief. "Then the CEO gets sick and Michael has to present the new strategy to the seventy-five senior managers by himself. When he does, they throw up all over the plan."

"How so?" I wanted specifics. The gorier the better.

"Well, I wasn't there, but Dick swore that one of the managers, the head of sales for Europe, a French guy, stood up and said something like, 'You American consultants have no idea how to approach the European market. This is one of the worst pieces of analysis I've ever seen, and I'm afraid that whatever we are paying your firm is too much.'"

I laughed. "Come on. That's hard to believe, even for a Frenchman."

"That's what I said when they told me, but they were adamant. And others at the meeting confirmed it."

"What did the rest of the executives in the room do?"

"That's the thing!" she said excitedly. "They did nothing! A few even piled on, saying that the direction of the company was all wrong. And half a dozen members of the executive team, all of whom were certainly more responsible for the actual input and decision about the company's strategy than Michael, sat there and didn't say a word."

"Michael must have been ticked off."

Amy took a second to think about it. "You know, he was definitely embarrassed. Or at least a little humiliated. But I don't think he was really all that angry."

"What did he say to the CEO and the other executives afterward?"

"That's the thing," Amy smiled. "He didn't really say anything. He just went back in there the next week and helped them put together a new plan."

I was starting to see an opportunity to lose some respect for Michael Casey, and I wasn't disappointed about that. Still, I tried to be tactful. "Isn't that a little weak?"

"That's exactly what I thought. Dick too."

This was too good to be true. There had to be a "but" coming. And there was.

"But when we asked him what he was going to do, he didn't seem to understand our question."

"What do you mean?"

"I mean, we asked him point blank, 'Are you going to go in there and tell those guys what a bunch of spineless jellyfish they are?' Heck, we figured Michael would want to walk away from a client for hanging him out to dry like that."

"So what did he say?"

Amy didn't hesitate this time. "I can remember what he said almost word for word: 'Listen, this is just an unpleasant part of our job sometimes. Those executives know that I took a bullet for them. I'll make sure they acknowledge that in some way, but I'm not going to punish them for it. Remember, they're paying us to help them make their company more successful, and if I had to be a trial balloon or a strategic piñata to make that happen, so be it.'"

I'm sure I rolled my eyes just a little, but Amy was watching the road and probably didn't notice. "What happened with the client?" I wanted to know.

"Well, the next time Michael met with the executives, they teased him about taking one for the team. So they knew what had happened. And then they asked Michael to help them figure out how to adjust the strategy."

"Did it work?"

Amy shrugged. "I don't know. I assume so, because the client is doing well today. And they became one of our most enthusiastic references. Their CEO probably brought us half a dozen other clients during the next five years."

I sat there in silence, watching brake lights mock me as we drove across the San Mateo Bridge.

Marty isn't going to want to hear any of this.

COUNSEL

I t was ironic that I was a strategy consultant, because what I needed most right then was a strategy of my own. I suppose Diane is my personal consultant, because she's the one I go to when I'm out of ideas.

"So explain the dilemma again," she invited me, without the slightest hint of impatience.

"It's complicated. Or maybe it's not. I don't know. Basically, there's something going on at this firm that is completely different from what happens at Kendrick and Black. I don't quite understand it all, but I'm pretty sure these folks come from a different planet."

"And why is that such a big deal?"

"Because my job is to integrate Lighthouse into K&B and then, if all goes well, take responsibility for running the practice. I don't know that either of those things is going to happen."

Diane looked a little stunned. "Whoa. Wait a second. Where is that coming from? You're a few weeks into this and you're already projecting problems that are way out on the horizon."

"Yeah, I realize it seems a little pessimistic."

"More like morose, but go on."

"Whatever. It's just that I'm okay at seeing around corners, and there's no way that Marty is going to buy into whatever it is that I'm learning here. He'd never want to work with these people, which means the acquisition will tank, I'll get tossed aside, my career will get thrown for a loop and ..." I paused, which gave Diane the opportunity she needed.

"You'll be sent to Siberia for fifteen years of hard labor, and then spontaneously burst into flames."

I would've laughed, except that was the line Diane always used with me and the kids when we were predicting doom. Instead, I pushed back. "Yeah, I know. I can deal with whatever happens. There's nothing to fear but fear itself. What doesn't kill you makes you stronger."

Diane was just a little annoyed now. "Are you saying that my advice is that stale? Because I don't think I—"

"No, no. It's not that. I'm just stuck."

"Okay, here's what you're going to do, Mr. High-Priced Management Consultant. I've said this to you before but you're going to spend the next few months learning everything you can about this firm, and you're going to enjoy yourself doing it. Goodness gracious. Can't you just find a way to like these people?"

"It's not that I don't like them."

"Okay then. You've got that going for you. So learn everything you can, present it all to Marty, and then let the chips fall—" She caught herself before finishing the cliché. "You know what I mean. Let whatever happens happen. Maybe Marty will grow a little here."

We both laughed. She went on, "Okay, so he's not going to grow. But he's going to want to make this work for himself, so it's not like he doesn't have some vested interest."

Then she brought out the big guns. "Besides, do you think God put you on this earth to worry about how to keep people like Marty and Jim Kendrick happy? Do your best, speak your mind, and stop worrying about things before they happen."

I took a breath. "You know, you should write one of those self-improvement books that people keep in the bathroom for when they have a few minutes to themselves."

Diane threw a pillow at me. "Hey, you're lucky I don't charge you for my advice, buddy."

I laughed and, as usual, decided to follow most of my wife's counsel.

ENDURANCE

For the next five weeks I pretty much threw myself into the day-to-day business of Lighthouse Partners, and I deflected Marty's occasional e-mails and phone calls with trite and general answers sprinkled with enough criticism of Half Moon Bay to keep him in the dark about what I was really thinking.

Gradually, I became more involved in the consulting and decision making, but always in unspoken deference to Dick and the others. By my sixth week, I had taken on two of my own clients, working with Matt on one of them and with another relatively young guy on the other.

I'm more than a little embarrassed to admit that it wasn't until I was almost two months into my Lighthouse experience that I came to realize something that should have been obvious—I was doing almost no selling!

At K&B I had spent as much as 60 percent of my time preparing for, delivering, and following up on sales calls. I had come to enjoy the gamesmanship of selling, but suddenly I wasn't missing it anymore.

I also came to the realization that this lack of formal selling was the primary cause of the financial gap between Lighthouse and K&B, and it had a much bigger impact than fees or salaries did.

Almost all of the time and energy in Half Moon Bay was being directed toward consulting to paying clients. Those clients in turn became the sales engine for the firm, and even when we did an occasional cold call, it was the references from clients that shortened the sales cycle considerably. I'm not even sure I'd call it a sales cycle at all.

As I approached the twelfth week of my integration project, Marty decided it was time to evaluate our progress and begin the process of more formal integration. I pushed him off for a week, and then another, until he started to get annoyed and insisted that we get together "next week." I relented and scheduled the meeting. And when he told me that Jim Kendrick and two additional partners from the managing team would join us, I started to get even more nervous.

With less than a week to prepare, I began assembling my notes and asking more pointed questions than ever about Michael Casey and his various rules of thumb that, more than anything, defined his approach to client service and business. I was also starting to see a few patterns connecting many of those points.

As I put together my thoughts for the meeting at K&B, I decided that talking to Marty and Jim Kendrick and the other partners about culture would be about as popular as leading them in a session of hot box yoga (to be honest, I don't really know what that is). And yet I was at a loss for how to convey what I had been learning. There was no way around it—this was going to be an ugly meeting.

And then something happened that made me question whether I should go to the meeting at all.

It was my first opportunity since joining Lighthouse to do a solo project for a client. That's when I was reminded that there is a big difference between understanding something and putting it into practice.

TEST RUN

Had just begun working with a small hospital located in Morgan Hill, a semi-agricultural town south of San Jose.

St. Therese de Lisieux Regional Medical Center had been founded by an order of nuns, a few of whom still served on the board. They had hired us to help them decide whether to expand or to open a new satellite facility to serve their patients who lived in some of the more remote areas further south.

I had met with the CEO of the hospital a few weeks earlier to scope out the project, and we decided that I should spend a full day with three or four of her executives and try to come to a decision. Though I had grown accustomed to the Lighthouse method of doing collaborative, real-time client research rather than preparing an answer ahead of time, I couldn't resist looking at my old files to get ready for the meeting.

I had worked with plenty of hospitals in my career, at both K&B and the medical device company where I spent three years after business school. Most of those were larger and more sophisticated facilities than St. Therese's, so I figured there was no reason not to use my prior knowledge with this client.

So I found my files and reviewed them, paying particular attention to cost analysis associated with multisite hospitals. By the time the working session came around, I felt confident that I'd be able to help them, and that there would be plenty of low-hanging fruit for me.

The hospital CEO, Michelle Thomas, introduced me to the handful of executives who would be holed up in the third-floor conference room for the next nine hours. Then she clarified the purpose of the day. "We are going to sit here for the next nine hours, or as long as it takes, until we figure out what makes sense in terms of expansion. And while I'm sure there are plenty of opinions and emotions at play here, let's make sure that we make our decision based on what makes the most sense long term."

With that, she handed it over to me.

I had already sized up the room and decided that the group probably had never made a decision like this before, and most likely they didn't have the analytical horsepower or experience to grasp all the variables that would be necessary. So I decided to start with my own hypothesis about what the ultimate answer would be and work backward from there. I guessed that we would be done by ten o'clock, if not sooner.

"Okay, I worked with a hospital in Bend, Oregon, a few years ago, Good Shepherd Medical Center, that was roughly the same size as St. Therese's and served a community not unlike yours. In addition to rebranding and cost management, we helped them sort through a similar decision about satellite expansion, and we came up with a model that I think might be helpful for us."

I pushed a button on the overhead projector to reveal a graph that I had used with my Oregon client.

"The team at Good Shepherd was pretty adamant about growing and establishing new facilities in outlying areas, both to serve patients there and fend off competitive threats. But as you can see, the data made it very clear that it would have been financially irresponsible to do so."

The eclectic group of executives stared at the chart far longer than it would have taken to digest its data. I realized that they were not merely digesting it intellectually, but coming to terms with the idea of not building the satellite facility, and possibly not growing at all.

For the next ninety minutes I answered question after question about Good Shepherd and my model and my background and my confidence that my client in Oregon had made the right decisions. Though the questions were asked without accusation or frustration, it was impossible not to detect the disappointment in the room.

As the conversation began to slow, it became apparent to me that the audience was coming to terms with the reality before them. All except one of them.

He was the oldest of the group, the chief medical officer, Dr. Something, but I think his first name was Carl. He was an OB-Gyn by trade and still practiced part-time. Like most labor and delivery doctors, he seemed like a nice guy, but I could tell he wasn't satisfied.

"Okay, I'm no accountant, and I certainly didn't learn anything about business strategy during my residency, but I just don't feel convinced by this." He paused and looked directly at me. "I'm not questioning your integrity, or anything."

I smiled and shook my head as if to say it's okay if you do.

He continued, "But given the population growth in the area and the lack of competition, I just can't imagine why we couldn't make this work."

I started to say, "Well, sometimes—" but he interrupted me.

"Just a second, Jack, I'm not quite finished."

He wasn't trying to be rude, I was sure. But it stung a little nonetheless.

"Our occupancy rate here is not at capacity, but it's higher than it's ever been and seems to be growing. Within a couple of years, we're going to be turning people away. Something just doesn't add up here."

To my credit, I forced myself to be gracious and avoid the slightest hint at condescension, though I would have liked to have said *Listen pops, you stick to pap smears, and I'll do the financial analysis.*

What I actually said was, "I understand where you're coming from. And what you're saying is exactly what some of the folks up at Good Shepherd said when they saw this. But when they went through the numbers, even with the potential for growth, it just wasn't feasible."

The doctor frowned, but not in a combative way. It was as though he was looking at a patient and trying to decide what was causing their pain. And like a good doctor, he wasn't about to give up.

"So you're telling me, Jack, that someone else isn't going to come into this valley and put up a new hospital in the next five years? Last year Kaiser almost did, and then they had to

109

retreat because of their own internal issues, but not because of anything having to do with this market."

At the time I was proud of myself for not letting the doctor fluster me. In the past, I would have made sure he understood the differences in our levels of expertise, and I would have pummeled him with data. Instead, I tried to reassure him.

"This is a complicated time in health care, and sometimes what seems like common sense actually makes no sense at all. I'm sure there are times when, as a doctor, you come to a conclusion that your patients just don't understand, and you have to trust in your training and expertise and experience."

He was nodding now, not necessarily convinced, but accepting my analogy. I was glad to have won him over without having to deliver a blow to his self-esteem. Who would have known that within the hour, it would be my self-esteem that would be on the ground?

HUMILITY

ichelle called for a break, and we all scrambled for a private space to make phone calls. I decided to see if I could track down one of the executives at Good Shepherd. Luckily, he was in his office, and I convinced his assistant to interrupt him for a quick conversation.

I asked him about the decision we had helped them make, and how it had turned out, and he confirmed that though they were initially skeptical, it had proved to be the right one. We then spent a few minutes reminiscing about the late nights we had spent on that and other projects, and then he jokingly said something innocuous that rocked my world.

"Between the expansion project, the cost-cutting, and the profitization work you did, I think you must have racked up quite a few points at the Hilton up here."

Somehow I was able to laugh politely at the comment and thank my old client for his time. But inside I was experiencing that sensation I had when I realized that my zipper was down for the first half of the prom, and that Christine Owens must have noticed. I wanted to go back in time and erase the past two hours and start over. And for that matter, go back twenty years and zip up my tuxedo pants.

The word that triggered all of this adolescent angst was "profitization." In fact, I don't think it's a word at all, but something we made up with the folks at Good Shepherd. In any case, it had to do with transforming the hospital from a non-profit to a for-profit, and I had completely forgotten about that part of my work there.

The problem, of course, was that St. Therese's was a non-profit hospital. This meant that the model I had been using was at best incomplete, and at worst, completely wrong.

I tried to convince myself that there was a way out of this dilemma. *Maybe the models aren't really that different, and the final conclusion will be the same.* I decided that if I could postpone the meeting for a half hour or so, I could find the right model, rerun the numbers, and figure out whether any of this mattered.

I went back to the conference room a little earlier than everyone else, and confirmed for myself, just to be sure, that I had, indeed, used the wrong model.

"Crap!" I said out loud.

And so I thought about how I would convince my clients to take an extended break that would give me the time to do a Houdini and somehow pull myself out of the fire.

When Michelle and the rest of the group returned, something horrible happened. Dr. Something, or Carl, came up to me, shook my hand, thanked me for helping them, and then, to make matters worse, complimented me. "Jack, it's clear that you are very good at what you do. It's always a treat for me to watch someone who has mastered their craft."

I wanted to cry.

SWALLOWING
MEDICINE

Holding myself together, I thanked Carl for his comment. When he returned to his seat, I stood up and did something I had never done before.

"Okay, I have an announcement to make." I paused and everyone quieted down. "I'm afraid that everything I've shown you so far may have been wrong."

I certainly had their attention now.

"The model I used for the analysis was based on a for-profit hospital. I completely forgot that Good Shepherd changed their profit status the year before we did the expansion study. These numbers are certainly wrong, and I wouldn't be surprised at all if my conclusions are way off." I paused. "I can't tell you how embarrassed I am."

In a matter of seconds the looks on the faces of the people in front of me seemed to morph from disbelief to disappointment to frustration, and then, to my astonishment, to consolation. And it was my new friend the doctor who went first.

In the kindest voice imaginable he said, "Well, I'd say you should be embarrassed, son."

Now, I hadn't been called "son" in years, but it certainly applied, because I felt like a nine-year-old boy.

He went on. "So what is your hourly rate, Jack? Because I think you owe us double that because we've just wasted two hours."

The people in the room burst out in laughter.

"Let's make him buy lunch!" Michelle chimed in.

I took my wallet from my hip pocket and threw it into the center of the table, and everyone laughed. At me. With me. I'm not sure. But it wasn't half as bad as I had imagined.

After the humor started to fade and the reality of the situation returned, I decided to push forward down this same road. "Okay, I can't believe I made such a ridiculous mistake. But I think we can salvage the day and still arrive at the right decision before midnight."

They laughed, and one of the analysts piled on. "Then you're going to be buying us dinner, too."

I smiled and accepted the punishment. "I'm going to need about twenty or thirty minutes to redo my analysis, and by lunchtime I'll have some preliminary numbers."

"What does your gut tell you the answer will be?"

It was the doctor who asked.

I gave it some thought. "My gut tells me that if you really think your occupancy numbers are going to continue growing and that the economic development in this area is not a fluke, expansion probably makes sense. But I'm guessing it would be here at the main facility, not in the satellite communities."

"Why is that?" Michelle wanted to know.

"Because most of my hospital clients—" I paused to qualify myself. "Though I'm not saying it would be exactly the same here, most of them find that there are so many redundancies and inefficiencies in satellite sites that it would be more cost effective to pay for free patient shuttles than it would be to build remote facilities."

"What about competition? Wouldn't we be exposed?"

"I don't think so. If you grow enough here, I think you'll be fine. You might see some remote labs and walk-in emergency centers come into the market here and there, but not enough to warrant a major financial investment on your part."

Unbelievably, they were nodding their heads as though they might actually believe anything I would say. I wanted to set their expectations lower. "But we'll know more after we do the analysis and discuss what you're seeing in the community. I could be way off." I don't think I had ever said anything like that to a client during my five years at K&B.

With that, we took a break. As Carl walked by me on his way to the door, he didn't say anything, but patted me on the shoulder, which meant more than he could have known.

Personal growth might not be so bad after all, I decided.

PREPARING THE
WITNESS

The rest of the afternoon and evening at St. Therese's was intense, exhausting, and difficult. And I had never enjoyed a day of consulting more in my life!

I challenged them. I argued with them. I changed my mind four times. I made mistakes. I had some great insights. I learned a lot about hospitals that I thought I already knew. I even served them pizza, and I cleaned up the conference room after we were done eating.

When we wrapped things up a little after eight o'clock, there was no doubt in our minds that building a new outpatient wing at the hospital was the right strategy. I seem to have a painful and suppressed memory of two of the team members high-fiving each other at one point.

As I drove home that night, I felt a strange mix of euphoria and dread. Euphoria about coming to terms with a new way to be a consultant and feeling like I was actually part of the team I had just helped. And dread that it might all come to an end on Monday morning when I met with Marty and Kendrick.

Fortunately, it was the weekend, which would give me a chance to regroup.

As usual, it was at church on Sunday that I had an epiphany, and I began to feel better about what would transpire during the next thirty-six hours. It's hard to remember exactly what happened during mass that changed my outlook. It was a mixture of the Bible readings, which so often seem to be chosen for exactly what I needed to hear; the sermon, which on this Sunday was about finding joy in suffering and trial; and just sitting there with my wife and kids and wondering how I had become such a wuss. And of course there was prayer.

Before bed that night, Diane asked how I was feeling about everything, and I told her that I was actually looking forward to the meeting, and that I had no idea what would happen. Though I had expected her to say "Way to go, tiger" or something perhaps a little less cheesy, she shocked me with two simple words: "Be careful."

She might as well have said "You're screwed big time, buddy!" because in that moment my confidence started to fade.

"What do you mean by that?"

Diane caught herself. "Nothing. It's just, well, nothing. You'll do fine."

It was too late. "No, you're not going to get away with that. What did you mean when you said 'be careful'?"

She hesitated. "Well, it's just that I don't want you to be so confident that you, I don't know, say something unnecessary and get into a weird situation."

I was partly exasperated, partly amused. "A weird situation?"

"It's just that you have a good job, and you've worked hard to get where you are ... "

She didn't finish the sentence, and I knew it was my turn to be the consultant in the relationship.

"Listen, Diane, we're going to be fine. I'm sure that I can make this integration work and that everything will turn out better than we could have imagined. Marty isn't exactly a Boy Scout, but he's not Darth Vader either."

She smiled. "I know. I'm sorry. I shouldn't have said anything."

I assured her that it was okay—and quietly wished I believed half the things I had just said.

PART FOUR

Testimony

TRIAL

As I nervously rode the same elevator to the twentieth floor where I had been going to work uneventfully for the past five years, I decided that I had probably overdramatized the magnitude of this meeting and the situation in general.

Jim Kendrick's opening comments at the meeting made it clear that I had not.

"We paid real money for this firm. What I want to understand today is what kind of return we're going to get." That was it. Classic Kendrick.

The setting could not have been any more ominous, like something right out of a movie. We were in the most formal conference room in the building, the one with a mahogany table and expensive black leather chairs. It provided a straight-ahead view of Alcatraz, which seemed appropriate.

Kendrick was sitting at one end of a table that could easily accommodate ten people. Janet Neves, the head of the firm's financial consulting division who was in town from New York, sat at the other end, flanked by another partner whose name I can't, for the life of me, recall. But I do remember that he looked like the Penguin, Batman's nemesis, but without the top hat.

I took one of the middle seats, leaving plenty of room between me and my superiors.

Marty, sitting directly across from me, didn't react at all to his boss's opening remark, but left me to respond on my own, as though this acquisition had been my idea all along.

So this is how you're going to play it. Maybe he was Darth Vader after all.

"Okay. I guess I'll go first. If you're asking what the specific financial impact of the acquisition will be, I can tell you right now that I have no idea." I paused for effect, deciding to milk the drama for whatever it was worth. "But if you're interested in what kind of benefits we might be able to get out of it, I can certainly speak to that."

Surprisingly, Janet Neves responded first. She was an extremely tall woman, maybe six feet plus, and she always wore pin-striped suits that made her look even taller. Her demeanor matched her clothes. All formality. "Well, I'm assuming we'll be able to monetize any of the nonfiscal benefits you address here."

I didn't know whether I needed to answer this ambiguous, jargony question or not, but before I could, Marty jumped in. "Absolutely. I think Jack's point is that it's too early to know exactly how this will impact our financials. That's all."

Janet nodded as though Marty had said something insightful, and it was then that it occurred to me how much I had enjoyed being away from K&B these past few months.

"Can you tell us about what you've learned since you've moved your office down to Half Moon Bay, Jack?" Suddenly Marty wanted to facilitate the meeting, no doubt to put himself in a position to ask questions rather than having to answer them.

I took a breath. "Okay, why don't we just get right to the point? You guys want to know how we're going to integrate Lighthouse and how that's going to make us stronger as a firm."

Kendrick seemed to like the direct approach and nodded approvingly. Unfortunately, he wasn't going to like what I had to say next.

"Well, I think this could be an extraordinary opportunity for Kendrick and Black, much bigger than I would have imagined a few months ago when the deal was announced."

Wait for it.

"But I'm not going to lie to you. We're going to have to work hard to learn how to do what they do."

It took more than a few seconds for my words to sink in with the shiny people sitting around the table. Marty went first.

"Did you say that we're going to have to learn how to do what they do?"

Without the slightest hint of sarcasm, humor, or defensiveness, I nodded my head. "That's right."

Kendrick was certainly engaged now. "You're going to have to explain this one, son."

It was the second time in a few days that someone had called me son. Suddenly I felt like the Tom Hanks character in the movie *Big*.

Marty was starting to look uncomfortable, which, I must admit, I found slightly enjoyable.

I dove in. "From a financial standpoint, Lighthouse has slightly better profit margins than we do, and slightly higher revenue per client."

"That doesn't mean we should be copying them," the Penguin countered. "They're a much smaller firm, and you can't really compare apples to—"

I couldn't help but interrupt: "You're right. It isn't a fair comparison." He seemed pleased by my response. Until I finished.

"We should be blowing them out of the water. We have hundreds of smiling college grads running around here all hours of the night who think they're well paid until they calculate their hourly compensation and realize they're earning a little more than minimum wage."

Even Janet chuckled.

I wanted to clarify my point. "Don't get me wrong. I realize that's the way consulting firms like ours make money. I'm not trying to be Norma Rae here."

Kendrick pushed on. "How many junior analysts or consultants do they have?"

I didn't hesitate. "They have Mary."

"Mary?"

"Yeah, she's the only consultant at Lighthouse under twenty-six years of age. Everyone else is pretty much an adult. It's unbelievable."

Janet was puzzled. "So why are their numbers so strong? Their salary per employee must be high."

"It is," I confirmed.

"Are their fees higher than ours?"

"A little. But not much."

Kendrick was beside himself now. "Wait. Did you just say that their fees are higher than ours?" He looked at Marty. "Why aren't we charging more?"

Under pressure now, Marty didn't have time to carefully formulate a politically correct answer. So he was uncharacteristically honest. "There is no way we can even think about increasing our fees right now. If anything, we're getting more pushback than ever about them being too high."

Kendrick turned to me. "Then how are they charging so much? And why aren't their clients complaining?"

"Before I get into that, let me make it clear that the fee differential isn't the big issue here. It's merely a symptom, and it's not even the most important one."

"Then how do you explain the financial discrepancy?" Janet wanted to know.

"It's all about their cost of sales."

"Explain." Kendrick was impatient.

"They spend almost none of their time selling."

Marty was getting increasingly annoyed and nervous, which would have been fine except that I was the only one in the room he could take it out on. "Then what have you been doing over there for the past four months?" It wasn't a question as much as an accusation.

I was caught off guard and struggled to defend myself. "Well, I've been—"

Kendrick cut me off: "Forget about that. I want to know what you mean when you say they aren't spending any time selling."

Deciding not to thank Kendrick for shutting my boss up, I regrouped and explained. "Well, most of their business comes from referrals and warm leads. And in the rare event that they do a cold call, they spend very little time doing research or writing up proposals or wordsmithing presentations."

"What do they do then?" Marty demanded to know.

I smiled, but barely. "They just show up."

I thought Marty was going to jump across the table and strangle me. "What's that supposed to mean?"

"It means that when they meet with a client they spend their time asking questions and doing primary research right there. It's like they skip the entire sales process. And they're remarkably successful."

I could see that my colleagues around the table were getting annoyed, so I went on the offensive a little.

"Listen, instead of trying to outsmart the companies they're selling to, they just go in there and start consulting. I've watched this a half dozen times now, and it's really incredible."

The dynamics in the room were as complicated as they were ugly.

It was clear that Kendrick was feeling a little embarrassed in front of his fellow partners, Janet and the Penguin. I would later find out that they had opposed the Lighthouse acquisition in the first place and wanted to hold Kendrick's feet to the fire.

Marty was all too aware of the fact that the wrath of Kendrick was about to come down on him. And I was pretty much in everyone's direct line of fire.

That's when Marty decided it was time to throw me under the bus. "If they're so good at this, then why aren't we doing it? You're the one responsible for sales in this division, Jack."

Normally, I would have melted in that situation. Today, all I could do was tell the truth. "That's the thing, Marty. It's not really about sales at all."

He was confused, but wasn't about to let me off the hook. "Well, it sure sounds like a sales issue to me."

Though no one else spoke, the looks on their faces made it clear that they agreed with him. It was all on the line for me now.

"That's what I thought when I first went down there. And then I saw how they worked with their clients. That is the biggest difference between us and them." I paused for effect. "And it's huge."

Kendrick frowned and looked squarely at me. "This better be good."

OFFENSE

At that point in the conversation, I could have sworn I heard Diane whispering *"Be careful"* in my ear. But somehow I could also hear her saying, *"Let 'em have it!"* I opted for somewhere in between. At least for the time being.

"Well, based on my observations during the last several weeks, I'd have to say that Lighthouse is far less professional than we are. They're also less sophisticated, less rigorous, and less systematic."

Marty seemed to breathe a sigh of relief.

"But they are so much more effective."

If I had been sitting in an ejector seat, that was the moment I would have been launched into San Francisco Bay. But because I was still firmly ensconced in my chair, I decided to keep going.

"Frankly, it's like they're in a completely different industry from the one we're in."

My audience was not about to take this lying down. Kendrick went first.

"Do you have any real evidence for what you're saying? Any data?"

"Data?" I was slightly incredulous. "Well, the numbers we talked about a few minutes ago are pretty good indications." Before he could counter, I continued, "But the real evidence can be found with their clients."

The Penguin now had a question. "You mean their clients' financial performance and stock price?"

I shook my head. "No, it's the fact that their clients love them so much."

Kendrick rolled his eyes.

"Don't you roll your eyes at me, old man!"

That's what I wanted to say. Instead, I wisely let it go.

The Penguin didn't. "What are you thinking, Jim?"

"Well, I don't know if we can really say with any degree of certainty that their clients' feelings about them are different from our clients' feelings about us."

I wasn't a brain surgeon, but I was pretty sure Kendrick was calling me a liar. Or at the very least, incompetent. Just in case that wasn't clear, he went on: "Again, do you have any data that substantiates this, Mr. Bauer?"

Mr. Bauer? Suddenly I wasn't a little boy anymore, but a defendant on trial. I decided that playing it soft was riskier than going for broke.

"Listen, every client I've spoken to raves about these people. They do most of the marketing for them, and without being asked. More than half their clients come from unsolicited referrals."

I could see they weren't buying it, so I pushed a little harder. "Come on, half of *our* clients won't agree to be a reference for us at all, and most of the others are less than enthusiastic when they do agree. Do you guys really think I'm lying to you here?"

And then I said something I would have thought impossible a few months before: "Do you really hate Michael Casey that much?"

Before Marty could say anything, Janet and the Penguin asked the same question, almost in unison: "Who's Michael Casey?"

Kendrick explained, "He's one of the founders of Lighthouse."

I added, "He's really the one who created the model for how they do business."

"So they have a model?" the Penguin wanted to know. "Can we see it?"

"Well, it's not so much a model ... " I hesitated. "They just operate on a set of informal principles."

Kendrick was done being nice. "Come on, Mr. Bauer, this is ridiculous. You're sitting here telling us that this little boutique consulting firm is so much better than we are, and that we have to learn to be more like them. And then you're telling us that you don't really know how they do it, that it's just an informal list—"

That's when I interrupted the man whose name was on my paycheck. And I wasn't being particularly meek. "No, I said *they* don't have a model." I paused. "But I've created one, and I think it captures what they do."

At that point I really thought that Kendrick would back down and ask me to explain the model.

I had underestimated his self-esteem, or lack thereof. He reacted as though he hadn't heard my previous sentence.

"So there's no real model. No data. No way of measuring the value of this deal to the firm. Do you have anything substantive?"

I sat there in silence for a moment, sensing that my credibility and career were eroding with every second that passed. Janet and the Penguin shuffled their papers to try to escape the uncomfortable situation.

I was desperate. "Give me a minute."

Before they could respond, I pulled the triangular speaker phone in the middle of the table toward me and dialed a number.

After just two rings, someone answered.

"Boxcar. How can I help you?"

Marty looked like he was going to kill me.

NO HOLDS BARRED

I couldn't let myself be distracted by my boss's fury.

"Is this Candace?"

"Yes, it is."

"Hi Candace, this is Jack Bauer."

I prayed that she wouldn't say "Who?"

"Hi, Jack. What can I do for you?"

"I need to talk to Gene."

Candace hesitated. "Let's see. Gene's in a budget meeting until four, but I can have him give you a—"

I interrupted, as politely as I could. "Actually, Candace, I need to speak to him right away."

She hesitated again, so I preempted her. "It's kind of an emergency. A huge favor." I hated having to say that in front of the people who were trying to skewer me.

She paused. "I'll do my best. Can you hold?"

I had no choice. "Sure."

While we waited anxiously, Marty tried to divert me. "What are you doing, Jack? Is this really appropriate? Calling a client?"

Kendrick and his peers seemed confused—and concerned.

I bluffed confidently, pretending to be dumbfounded by his questions. "Appropriate? Why not? It's fine. You'll see."

I didn't know how much time that would buy me. I half expected Marty to lean across the table and hang up the phone. Luckily, Candace had come through.

"Jack?"

It was Gene Kravets, the CEO of Boxcar.

"Hey, Gene. Thanks for taking my call. Sorry to interrupt your meeting."

"No problem. We needed to take a break anyway. What do you need?"

I hesitated and then decided there was no way to sugarcoat this. "Well, I'm trying to explain to a group of very interested people what it is that Lighthouse does and how it differs from Kendrick and Black."

"Okay."

"And since you recently chose Lighthouse over K&B, and even agreed to pay a higher retainer, I thought you would be able to articulate for us why you made that decision."

"Sure, I can do that. But it sounds like I'm on speaker phone. Do I have an audience?"

I hesitated again, thinking hard about how I could avoid answering this question. There was no way. "Yeah, I've got Janet Neves here, and Marty Shine, and the Penguin." Of course I didn't call him that. I suppose I must have known his name at that point. "And Jim Kendrick."

There was silence on the phone for a moment. "Did you say *Kendrick*?"

"Yeah, Jim Kendrick. The founder of our firm."

I could almost hear Gene smiling on the other end of the phone. "And you want me to tell you why I chose Lighthouse over Kendrick and Black?"

"That's right. And why you're okay with paying higher fees." I was wishing Diane could have been in the room, because I was sure she wouldn't believe any of this when I told her.

Gene Kravets wasn't quite ready to give me what I wanted.

"Can you tell me what the purpose of this is? I mean, how honest do you want me to be?"

Marty shot me another look, one that I briefly thought about capturing on my phone camera, but I decided it would have been weird. Besides, I needed to answer Gene's question.

"I'm asking you to be completely honest, Gene. In fact, I'm begging you. Now that we've acquired Lighthouse, we need to understand what they do so well."

"Are you sure?"

I looked at Jim Kendrick to solicit his permission, knowing that anyone with any integrity at all would have to welcome the truth, at least in public.

Jim cleared his throat. "This is Jim Kendrick, Gene, and I would appreciate complete candor here." I could tell he didn't mean it, but Gene didn't know any different.

"Okay then. Where do you want me to start?"

To my surprise, it was the Penguin who took the lead. "Why don't you just tell us why you made the decision you did?"

Gene paused, most likely to collect his thoughts. "Well, first of all, I should say that you guys compared well against some of the other firms we talked to. In fact, for a while there, it came down to you and Strategic Insights."

Strategic Insights was one of the relatively large competitors that K&B faced in most of our accounts.

"And we were just about to make our decision when I spoke to a guy I know who used to run a manufacturing company in San Jose, and he told me that I'd be crazy not to talk to Lighthouse. I had never heard of Lighthouse, but he gave me the number right there and even set up a conference call so he could make the introduction himself."

Kendrick, Janet, and the Penguin exchanged glances that seemed to be a mix of equal parts condescension toward Lighthouse, and jealousy and awe of their new acquisition and the enthusiasm of its clients.

Gene went on, "So, I had a fifteen-minute phone conversation with Dick Janice, and then I met with him and another consultant for an hour or so. And without even having to think about it, I knew we'd be working with them."

"What exactly happened during that meeting?" the Penguin wanted to know.

"Well, I'm not sure. I mean, it was like they made the decision for me. I wish I could explain it better than that. Trying to do this over the phone isn't easy."

Jim Kendrick changed the line of questioning. "Maybe you could tell us what the K&B people did during their sales call, and compare the two approaches."

"Okay. That would probably be helpful. I guess the people from your firm, Jack and someone else I don't remember—"

"Margaret Stevens," I reminded him.

"Right. Margaret. They were very nice, and competent, and came with a bunch of material already prepared about our industry and our competitors. They told us about the resources that your firm has, and about all the clients you've worked with. They showed us some of the work you did with another technology company that was about the same size as us. I mean, I had no doubt that they were smart enough and experienced enough to help us. And I can't say I was at all unhappy with what they said or did. Like I said before, we were going to go with you or Strategic Insights."

The Penguin pushed a little harder. "So can you remember anything specific about the Lighthouse meeting?"

"Yeah, I guess now that I think about it, I do remember being a little surprised that Dick didn't bring any collateral or handouts and didn't really do a presentation. In fact, it was obvious that they hadn't had time to do much research before the meeting, because they spent the first hour asking questions about our business and our competitors and our market."

Gene laughed. "You know, I'm betting that Jack and Margaret would have been able to answer those questions themselves."

I smiled. "Yes, we could have. But you didn't pick us. Why?"

"Well, since you asked me to be honest, I'm just going to say it straight." He paused. "It just felt like you guys were going to tell us how to run our business, and you were trying to convince us that you knew more than us, I guess. And you were telling us all the things that you would do for us if we hired you."

"Lighthouse didn't do that?" Marty asked.

"No. They just started doing it."

"Doing what?" Marty asked again.

"Helping us. Offering suggestions. Giving us advice."

Marty was getting a little impatient now. "But you just said they didn't know anything about your business."

Gene paused, and I could have sworn that if we could have seen him he would have been scratching his head. "Yeah, that's the thing. They didn't come with any answers. But they asked questions. And they had suggestions, but they admitted that some or all of those suggestions might not be right. And some of them weren't, but some were, and more than anything, it felt like they were more interested in helping us figure out our problems than they were in closing the deal."

Kendrick gave me a look that seemed to say *Hey, that's what you've been trying to tell us.* Or maybe he was just having gas. In any event, one of us should have felt better.

Before we could ask any more questions, Gene brought the conversation to a close. "Hey, I'd be glad to give you any more information you need another time. I'm going to have to get back to this meeting, though."

"One more question." It was Kendrick, and he didn't wait for permission to ask it. "What has it been like working with Lighthouse since then?"

"It's been the same."

"The same as what?"

"The same as it was that day. It's like all they're interested in doing is helping us solve our problems. I've already told half a dozen other CEOs about them. I couldn't be happier."

The Penguin stepped in. "Thanks for your time, Gene. And your business."

"No problem. Take care." And he hung up.

For a long five seconds, the room was dead silent.

"So, Jack, now we understand what you've been trying to tell us. You were right. We were wrong. And we never should have doubted you. Would you help us learn how to be more like Lighthouse so that we can become a better firm?"

And if you believe anyone said that to me, then I have some swampland to sell you.

The reality was far less pretty.

SUCKER PUNCH

arty got the bloodletting started.

"So, Jack, let's summarize this meeting. You've come here today to tell us that you don't really know what kind of value we're going to get from this acquisition, and that you don't know how we're going to integrate them because they're so much better than we are."

I could tell he was being sarcastic, so I didn't say "You betcha!" Instead, I just waited for what would come next.

"And the evidence you have for all this is one client who chose Lighthouse over Kendrick and Black, and the consultant that lost that deal for us was ..." He paused for dramatic effect. "You."

Looking back, I have to admit that what Marty did there was impressive, albeit in a slimy trial lawyer kind of way. After all the evidence that I had presented, he had somehow distorted it so that it seemed to condemn me.

My only hope was the jury. Unfortunately, they had a vested interest in one particular verdict.

"I'm going to have to agree with Marty on this one," Janet offered. "And I'm also going to have to say that putting a client on the spot like that was not a very professional thing to do."

The Penguin nodded his agreement.

I could not believe what I was hearing. I knew that these people were not idiots, so the only thing I could attribute their insane response to was a profound lack of courage and intellectual integrity.

I turned to Jim Kendrick in a last-ditch plea for reason. He looked at me with kindness and said, "This isn't your finest hour, is it Jack?"

After digesting, regurgitating, and redigesting his comment, I slowly pushed myself away from the table, stood, moved around to the back of the chair, pushed it under the table, and delivered a response that was superior to anything I could have come up with in two weeks of preparation.

"Not my finest hour? Did you just say that it's not my finest hour? I have spent the last four months behind enemy lines studying the methods of a company that we have been jealous of for years. It has been difficult and humbling and eye-opening. I have come here and tried to give you all an unvarnished account of what I've learned, and what we need to learn if we're ever going to rise above the transactional, sweatshop mentality that makes our employees, our clients, and even us weary."

And yes, I actually did say exactly that.

But I wasn't finished. I then looked directly at Darth Vader. "And you have the gall to suggest that somehow all of this is simply a matter of my own shortcomings as a consultant. Did you pay attention to anything that CEO just said? Or are you simply too proud, too afraid to admit that there might be a better way to do this?"

It was at that moment that Jim Kendrick showed his true colors. He was not about to let one of his minions get called on the carpet. "Why should we listen to you, Jack? Marty is right. You lost the account. I don't think you have any credibility here. If anything, you're the one who's in denial. What that CEO said was more a condemnation of you than of Kendrick and Black."

Ouch. If you had told me two months or two weeks or even two hours earlier that Jim Kendrick was going to say something that harsh to me in a meeting, I'd have considered quitting right there. But fortunately, I had purposely held back one vital piece of information, something that I had hoped to avoid using and should never have had to use. But they gave me no choice.

"Oh, but I do have credibility. What Gene said didn't condemn me at all."

Now Marty jumped back in. "How can you say that? The man just admitted that you couldn't sell—"

I interrupted him calmly, saying in a quiet, unemotional tone, "Dick Janice couldn't take on Boxcar and had to find someone else to run the account."

The people in the room didn't seem to understand what I was trying to say, so I made it clear. "The lead consultant on that project is me."

Marty froze. Janet, Kendrick, and the Penguin were suddenly speechless. Evidently they couldn't find the words, or the courage, to respond.

So I just walked out of the room.

DELIBERATION

As I made my way to the elevators, I had this cheesy hope that someone—Kendrick would have been my first choice—would come running after me, imploring me to come back and share my insights. A raise and a promise to fire Marty would have been nice too.

But life isn't a movie, and in the real world people have less courage and dramatic flair. So I rode the elevator down alone, balancing feelings of exhilaration, fear, and nausea.

The nausea subsided before I arrived home, and within fifteen minutes of talking to Diane, I realized that much of the fear was gone too.

"I don't care if they fire you and we have to move to North Dakota," Diane promised me. "What you did was awesome."

And the thing is, she meant it, which made all the difference to me. Still, I found myself obsessing about the fallout from the episode and the repercussions it would have on my career.

Spending time with my children before bed that evening had an interesting impact on my worries. On the one hand, it calmed me by giving me a sense of perspective about what mattered in life. On the other hand, it made me worry about my livelihood, which was primarily devoted to providing for them.

Needless to say, I didn't sleep well that night.

The next morning I woke up and wondered what I would do that day. Was I going to be fired? Should I just go back to Half Moon Bay and act like the previous day had never happened?

So I checked e-mail and found a note from Marty, which was certainly shorter and more cryptic than I would have liked.

From: Marty Shine
To: Jack Bauer
Subject: Lighthouse

Jack,

After you left, we spent more than an hour discussing the Lighthouse situation. We want you to come back today at noon to finish the conversation. We'll have lunch brought in. Call me if you can't make it.

Marty

I showed it to Diane.

"This is a good thing," she said. "They're definitely feeling bad about what happened. They just couldn't come right out and say it because they're too insecure."

I wanted to believe her, but I just couldn't. If that were the case, even a cretin like Marty would have put something marginally nice in the note.

So I got dressed and had breakfast, feeling a little like a prisoner getting ready for the gallows. I would never have guessed that Honey Nut Cheerios would be the choice for my last meal.

CROSS-EXAMINATION

When I arrived at the office, I learned that we would be meeting in a different conference room. I was somehow relieved not to be going back to what I would forever think of as the Alcatraz Room. My relief was short-lived.

I was sent down to the nineteenth floor, to a smaller, windowless conference room. As I walked in, I was shocked to see that all the chairs in the room—I think there were seven—were taken by the various partners who headed the assortment of departments located in the San Francisco office. There was Janet Neves, the Penguin, and a handful of others. But Marty and Jim Kendrick were nowhere to be seen.

Janet came over to greet me, and she got right to the point without even acknowledging what had happened the day before. "Okay, we'll have you present from the front of the room. At the whiteboard. You've got thirty minutes."

"To do what?" I asked.

"To go over this model, or whatever it is, that Lighthouse does."

I was confused. "And what's the goal here?"

She looked at me in a puzzled kind of way, as though I had asked her why she was so tall. "Well, the goal is to explain to these people what it is that Lighthouse does. You know. What we were talking about yesterday."

At that moment I was shocked to see Jim Kendrick enter the room, pushing a chair. He positioned it in one of the few remaining open spots in the crowded room and sat down.

My mind was reeling, but I had to pull myself together, because at that point Janet turned to the nicely dressed executives sitting around the table and announced, "Jack is going to tell us what he's learned about the way that one of our most recent acquisitions approaches consulting with their clients."

And she sat down.

I found myself smiling, but I was thinking *You people really are insane, aren't you?* Going to the whiteboard, I picked up a blue pen—blue is my favorite color—and turned to the audience, all of whom I had met before, but most of whom I knew only casually.

It would be a real understatement to say I was nervous, not to mention confused as to what I was going to do.

And then it hit me. *Don't tell them. Show them.*

I stood there slightly dazed by this simple realization. And suddenly the world looked very different. I dove in.

"As you may know, I've spent the last four months or so working with Lighthouse Partners, a relatively small boutique firm we acquired earlier this year. During that time I've seen some things that I've never seen before, in terms of how to work effectively with clients."

I turned toward the whiteboard but didn't know what to write, so I turned back to my audience again. Normally that would have been awkward, but suddenly I was in a place of quiet confidence, where *awkward* didn't seem to matter.

"Okay. Some of you may not know that Jim, Janet, the Penguin, and I had a fairly contentious meeting yesterday." I looked toward Jim, who looked decidedly surprised and uncomfortable that I was being so open about our ugly get-together in the Alcatraz suite. I didn't include Marty in my list of attendees because today he wasn't in the room.

"As you can probably imagine, this is a difficult situation for me. I mean, the fate of my career here at K&B pretty much lies in your hands, and I'm about to tell you why I think your firm, our firm, needs to change what we do."

It was astounding how much more comfortable I felt just being honest. So I kept going.

"And I realize that it would be natural for you to feel a little defensive about what I'm going to say, so I want to assure you that my only motivation here is to make the firm more successful. I'll admit that most of my comments are based on my observations and intuition, not on reams of data or rigorous statistical analysis. But I can stand here and tell you that I'm extremely confident about the conclusions I've drawn, and that I welcome any of your questions and pushback."

I couldn't believe it, but Janet actually smiled. Like she was proud of me, and wanted to reach down and pat me on the head. And I would have let her.

I took a breath and continued.

"Essentially, Lighthouse Partners uses a handful of principles that one of their founders, a guy named Michael Casey, put in place years ago. Based on what I've seen, these principles have created a more loyal and enthusiastic client base than anything I've seen, in any industry."

I could tell my audience's interest in what I was saying jumped a few notches. "And I'd like to tell you about those principles, and what I think lies beneath them."

Before I could dive in, one of the younger partners in the firm, Larry DeWitt, raised his hand. Larry ran the accounting and audit practice.

"I don't mean to be difficult," he began, meaning he was going to be difficult. "But why haven't I heard of Lighthouse Partners? If they're so good at this . . . " He didn't bother to finish the sentence.

"Well, they're definitely a boutique firm, and they do almost all of their work here in the Bay Area. From the beginning they wanted to keep the firm relatively small."

Before DeWitt could counter, one of the other executives in the room, a woman who ran the organizational consulting division, came to my defense.

"Our division certainly knows about Lighthouse," she said. "They've taken clients from us on more than one occasion. And I've heard stories about how good their consultants are."

DeWitt wasn't about to give up, trying with some success to hide his arrogance. "Still, when a company says they want to stay small, it's often an excuse for not knowing how to grow."

At that moment I felt like I wanted to passionately defend Michael Casey, a man I had never met and had loathed just a few months earlier. But not wanting to seem too biased, I did my best to be über-diplomatic. "Yeah, I know what you mean.

However, in this case the company really was purposeful about maintaining its size. The founder is a family man, first and foremost, and was determined to avoid letting his work ruin his home life."

The reaction to that statement surprised me. As I would have expected, a few of the partners glanced at each other subtly in a way that suggested they thought what I had said was *touchy-feely*. But a few of the others—and I'm sure I read their faces correctly—seemed to almost smile in admiration, even nodding their heads a little.

Bolstered by the untested assumption that some of the people in the room might actually be my allies, I then said something that, in retrospect, I could have phrased more delicately. "But I'd have to say that if they wanted to, Lighthouse could have scaled what they did into a much bigger firm. And that would not be have been a good thing for us."

Suddenly everyone in the room, including my potential allies, seemed to shift into defense mode, with a few of them laughing dismissively. And wouldn't you know it, Jim Kendrick spoke first.

"Now wait a second, Jack." He smiled and responded in a way that simultaneously seemed condescending and apologetic. I was just glad he didn't call me *Mr. Bauer* or *son*. "I think we could have held our own against them."

The people in the room seemed glad that their leader had defended them. I had to be careful.

"Well ..." I paused. "I'm not going to stand here and say that Kendrick and Black is not a great firm."

I felt a little dirty because, in fact, I didn't think K&B was a great firm. But I suppose in a technical sense my statement

149

wasn't a lie because I wasn't about to stand there and actually say it.

"But ..." I paused again and realized that, even if I had wanted to, it was too late to hold back what I was about to say next. "Pretty much every time we've come up against Lighthouse Partners over the past five years in a head-to-head sales situation, we've been beaten."

People didn't respond but glanced toward Kendrick to see how he would react. I decided I should continue before he could say anything.

"And don't get me wrong. I've been on the receiving end of their butt-kickings as much as anyone, and I learned to hate them for it."

Fortunately, my audience seemed to accept my sincere self-deprecation.

"But now I understand exactly how they were beating us and why it worked so well."

Kendrick didn't say a word, but I could see by the looks on the faces of the others in the room that I had finally earned my permission, albeit tentatively, to convince these people that I had something worthwhile to tell them.

I had twenty-five minutes to salvage my career. I can honestly say that I wasn't all that nervous. But then again, I had no idea what was going on.

MAKING THE CASE

I couldn't decide whether to start by telling them about Michael Casey's various principles or to go right into the model that I had come up with around them. I chose to go with my model, on the grounds that it was my own and I felt more comfortable explaining it with confidence. And I knew I needed to be confident.

"More than anything else, the power of what Lighthouse does can be explained by one word: *vulnerability*."

Okay, I wasn't expecting the room to burst into spontaneous applause. But neither did I expect anyone to mock me before I could explain. Which was exactly what my friend Mr. DeWitt did.

"Did you say vulnerability?" He smiled and didn't wait for me to respond. "Is this some kind of new-age hippy thing where we're going to get naked and hold hands?"

The room chuckled collectively, and I forced myself to laugh along with them. I even joined them in the skepticism. "Yes, and then we'll be smoking dope and singing Grateful Dead songs."

They laughed even more.

"But it's interesting that you used the word *naked*," directing my comment at Larry, "because that's not a bad way to describe the way Lighthouse presents themselves to clients."

I had their attention again. After writing "vulnerable" and "naked" on the board, I continued.

Vulnerable/Naked

"What I'm talking about here is a certain kind of fearlessness they have. Whether they're selling or consulting, they just don't seem afraid of anything."

The Penguin spoke next, not skeptically, but out of what seemed to me like genuine curiosity. "What would they be afraid of?"

"Three things," I said like a confident professor who had been baiting his students. I finally had them where I wanted them, and I was ready to unleash my model.

Suddenly I wondered if it made any sense and if I should have reviewed it with someone at Lighthouse first. Too late to worry about that, I decided, and dove in.

THE FIRST FEAR

"The first one is the fear of losing the business, either during the sales cycle or in the process of doing consulting. I think that's pretty straightforward." I wrote it on the board:

#1 Fear of losing the business

I was about to go on to the second of the three fears, when I turned and noticed that most of the partners were frowning—not cynically, but more in a way that suggested they were trying to understand my model.

"What do you mean by that? How can they not care about losing the business?" It was the Penguin again.

"Well, it's amazing to me how little anyone at Lighthouse worries about whether they're going to close a deal, or whether a client might decide to stop working with them."

Before I could explain further, Jim Kendrick spoke and shocked everyone—not by what he said, but by how he said it.

"Now, I'm sorry if this sounds cynical, Jack."

I'm pretty sure no one, including myself, had ever before heard Jim Kendrick say something so politely and genuinely.

He might as well have stripped to his boxers and started singing show tunes. Of course, I had no way of knowing if he was being sincere, because I had never witnessed him being particularly nice before.

He continued, "But how can they be good consultants if they don't care about keeping their clients?"

No longer fretting about my children's college fund, I confidently stayed true to my own naked approach. "That's a good question, Jimbo." (Oh, come on. You know I didn't say "Jimbo.") "It's not that they go out of their way to tick off their clients. It's just that they're so focused on saying and doing whatever is in the best interests of those clients that they stop worrying about the repercussions. They make themselves completely vulnerable, or naked, and don't try to protect themselves."

My audience seemed to be trying to decide whether to accept my ideas or pick them apart. I was grateful when Janet asked the first question:

"Can you give me an example of this?"

Moving back toward the whiteboard in anticipation of needing to write something down, I began by explaining the difference between how Lighthouse goes about doing sales calls and how Kendrick and Black does it.

The new members of my audience, those who hadn't been with us in the Alcatraz room the day before, were dumbfounded by Lighthouse's lack of preparation and rigor during the sales process.

"So, you're saying that they don't do research before they start selling?" Larry asked.

"Well, they'll usually look at a company's website and get a general sense of what business the client is in. But they do most of their research when they meet the client, by asking questions. And they certainly don't come with a slideshow or a marketing packet."

I'm pretty sure Larry thought that I was an alien. "And the clients respond to that? I'd think they'd be unimpressed, if not insulted."

"You know, they might be. But only at first. It's not like they're going to kick a consultant out of their office in the first five minutes for being unprepared. Once they spend some time with the Lighthouse folks, I think they forget about their initial impression and are disarmed by their ..." I struggled for the right phrase, and settled on "humble self-confidence."

Now the Penguin jumped in, a little impatiently. "Even after our meeting yesterday, this is still too vague for me."

Feeling virtually no discomfort, I explained, "Well, two of Michael Casey's first rules of thumb are to be a consultant and not a salesperson, and to give away the business." I wrote both of these on the board:

> Consult, don't sell.
> Give away the business.

"What they mean is that you shouldn't try to sell to a client by telling them what you would do for them if they hire you. You should just start consulting right then and there."

"But what if you give them a great idea, and they decide they don't need to hire you and that they can just use the idea themselves?" Larry asked.

"I wondered the same thing myself when I first went to Lighthouse. But in reality, it almost never happens. I mean, sure, if all a client is looking for is one idea, then you'd be better off just giving it to them and letting them burn you and get it over with. But in reality, clients want someone who not only has good ideas, but who also will help them implement them. Which, when you think about it, makes sense."

Larry nodded, acceding the point to me.

I went on, "The other part of this, giving away the business, is about never worrying about the fees. Don't bring them up during the sales call unless they ask. Don't apologize for what you charge when they do ask. And if there's ever a dispute about fees, side with the client and charge the lesser amount."

Janet frowned at me. "That sounds like a recipe for being taken advantage of."

"Exactly. That's what nakedness and vulnerability are all about. If a client wants to take advantage of you, let them."

"I'm confused," Kendrick announced, echoing what seemed to be on the minds of most of the others in the room. "Yesterday you said that these people charge higher fees than we do. And now you're saying they let clients underpay them."

I smiled. "That's the crazy thing. Most of their clients would never even think of underpaying them. Which makes sense, because once a client trusts you and really understands that you care more about them than about yourself, they usually stop worrying about micromanaging the cost or seeing if they can take advantage of you."

156

One of the other partners raised his hand but didn't wait to be called on. "Is Lighthouse ever tempted to take advantage of clients? To pad the bills?"

I was shaking my head before he finished the question. "Never. That would be selling their soul to the devil. In fact, I've seen consultants at Lighthouse go to a client and suggest that they pay a lower retainer because they weren't using their services enough."

At least half the room gave me a look that said, *We don't believe that for a second.*

I insisted. "I know it sounds insane, but I saw it with my own eyes. These people are nuts." I laughed, and so did most of the others in the room. "It's all about standing there naked in front of the client. It's about building trust. And in the end, that means the client trusts them and takes care of them."

Now a few more of the partners were taking notes, and I knew that I was making progress. But there was more to the fear of losing the business yet to explain, not to mention the other two fears, so I pushed on.

"Okay, another one of Michael Casey's rules of thumb related to overcoming the fear of losing the business is something he calls 'telling the kind truth.'"

Tell the kind truth.

"This might be the most powerful of all the things they do. It's something that I was never taught in my career, and it doesn't come easy. But it's key to their success."

One of the partners who hadn't spoken yet, a roundish guy with suspenders named Finley (I don't know if that was his first or last name), offered his first comment. "This sounds a little like kindergarten talk to me."

Though I wasn't put off by the comment, the rest of the room seemed to be. It felt like Finley had drained a little of the goodwill that I had been building up, and, given that it was his first interaction with me, I think they were embarrassed for him. Even I felt bad for the guy.

"Well, there is nothing kindergarten-like about what this looks like in practice. In fact, it can be brutal."

They seemed anxious for me to explain, so I went on. "I know a consultant at Lighthouse who told his client that he needed to move his son out of a leadership position because he was incompetent. Another guy I know recently told a CEO that he doesn't hold his staff accountable. And last week I had to tell a guy that I thought he talked too much during meetings. But remember the 'kind' part. We give them that sort of feedback with a level of empathy and concern that you would normally reserve for a friend."

"I thought you said this wasn't going to be touchy-feely," Larry challenged me.

"Touchy-feely? Are you kidding?"

"Yes. I'm kidding." Larry smiled, and the others laughed. I was relieved, but Finley pushed back.

"I think we've all had those kinds of conversations with clients, Jack. You might be building these consultants up a little too much."

I was prepared for that objection, but I didn't want to be too tough and crush my suspender-wearing colleague.

"That may or may not be the case. But I have to tell you, the frequency with which these people do this is beyond anything I've ever seen in this business. And the response they get from those clients is ridiculous."

"Ridiculous how?" the Penguin wondered out loud.

"In terms of the level of appreciation they get. No matter how uncomfortable the conversation might be in the moment, eventually the clients are so glad that someone cares enough about them to be honest—"

Janet Neves completed my point. "They probably can't imagine not having you around."

I smiled and nodded. "Exactly."

As a few of the partners were writing this down, Jim Kendrick spoke. "Can you move on to the other two fears? We've only got fifteen minutes."

I looked at the clock. "Oh crap."

They laughed.

"There is one more part of the fear of losing the business that you need to understand. It's probably my favorite one."

I went to the board and wrote,

Enter the danger.

"Okay, this one comes from the world of improvisational theater. Or at least that's what my wife tells me. The idea is that when a group of actors are doing improv, and one of them says something particularly bizarre, it's important for the others to avoid the tendency to dodge or ignore that comment, but instead to walk right into the middle of it.

159

That's where the best improv comes from—the wackiest, most uncomfortable stuff."

I think the people in the room might have known where I was going, but I had to finish the point.

"In consulting, entering the danger comes into play in those moments when you're in a meeting and someone says something that is either strange or politically sensitive, and you know that the level of anxiety and discomfort in the room is high. What you're tempted to do is just be quiet and let the moment pass, but what great consultants do, at least according to Lighthouse, is walk right into the middle of the situation and call it out."

No one was writing this down, so I continued.

"I've seen this plenty of times in the last few months, and I've even done it myself. It's terrifying and uncomfortable. And clients absolutely love it."

Larry squinted and shook his head. "Wait a second. I can see that this might be a good thing, but how can you say with any degree of certainty that clients love it?"

"This is a serious question, right? I just want to make sure you're not kidding again."

They laughed.

"Yes, I'm serious. I mean, it's one thing to say—"

I interrupted. "No, it's okay. I understand. You want to make sure I'm not exaggerating this stuff. I get it."

He nodded his head in a somewhat conciliatory way, so I answered.

"Whenever I see someone enter the danger—and that includes the one time I did it—clients inevitably come up to you individually and thank you. They say things like 'I'm so glad you made us talk about that,' and 'I've been wanting to do what you did today for three years, but I felt like it would have been a career-limiting move.'"

A light went on just above Janet's head. "So you have to be confident enough to do something that is potentially client-threatening." It was sort of a question.

I wanted to go up to her, step up on my tippy toes, and give her a big kiss. Instead, I just said, "Yes."

Jim Kendrick interrupted, impatiently but not cynically, which I'll take from him any day. "Okay, can you move on to the second one, whatever you call it?"

The Penguin helped him. "Fear. The second fear."

"Right," Kendrick acknowledged. "Can you move on to the second fear? We're running out of time here."

Thrilled by the idea that my audience was actually interested in what I was saying, I gladly obliged.

THE SECOND FEAR

"he second fear that Lighthouse doesn't have—and one that most consultants, including myself, struggle with—is the fear of being embarrassed or looking stupid in front of their clients."

#2 Fear of being embarrassed

I didn't wait for a question. "Now, I'm not saying that they go out of their way to look stupid, or have no filter on what they say to their clients, but when in doubt, they speak up. And as painful as that is in the moment, it is disarmingly effective in terms of adding value and endearing them to their clients."

"Do you have an example, Jack?" Suddenly Finley was sounding friendlier. And I couldn't help but wonder if suspenders were more comfortable for a large guy than a belt. Stay focused, I thought to myself.

"Yeah. But they fall into a few different categories. And again, these are Michael Casey's principles or rules of thumb."

I went to the board and wrote,

Ask dumb questions.

"When a Lighthouse consultant doesn't understand something, they always probe. Whether it's an industry term or an acronym or a concept that everyone else in the room seems to understand, they just never pretend to know more than they do. And I have to admit that when I'm sitting there too afraid to ask what I think might be a stupid question, and then one of my colleagues does, I always admire them and feel like a wuss for not asking it myself. And I think their clients appreciate that about them."

Not quite satisfied, Kendrick asked, "Specific examples?"

"Let's see." I took a minute to stare at the whiteboard, as though I would find a good story written in magic spy writing there. "It's hard, because this happens all the time and usually it's not all that interesting."

Then something occurred to me. "I suppose the dumbest question I've heard about came from Amy Stirling, one of the senior partners at Lighthouse. As the story goes, and I heard it straight from her, she was in a strategy session with some executives from the San Francisco 49ers football team. Now, Amy isn't a big sports fan and knows next to nothing about football. So they're in the middle of a conversation about marketing and reviving the team's brand by reconnecting with the team's history, when someone suggests they use Jerry Rice in their advertisements. After a few comments from others in the room, Amy raises her hand and asks, 'Who is Jerry Rice?'"

Most of the room broke out into laughter.

163

Janet Neves smiled and shook her head. "Come on. Even I know who Jerry Rice is!"

I defended my story. "I've talked to people who were in the room at the time, and they swear it happened."

"What did the 49er executives do?"

"Well, for a second they sat there stunned, thinking that Amy was kidding. And then when they realized she was serious, I guess they razzed her pretty good. At the end of the meeting, someone even gave her a signed Jerry Rice jersey, just to rub it in. But she recovered."

I worried that my audience would somehow think that my Lighthouse colleagues were ignoramuses, so I qualified my story. "Now remember, unlike that particularly egregious case, usually when one of the consultants asks a dumb question at least one other person in the room admits that they don't know the answer either. And then the consultant looks like a hero."

Goodwill or not, Kendrick was still impatient. "What else do you have for us?"

I went to the board. "Well, similar to asking dumb questions, they believe in making dumb suggestions."

Make dumb suggestions.

"I've seen people do this quite a few times too."

"Examples?" Kendrick asked.

I had to think about it for a moment. "Let's see. Do you want a really dumb one, or an idea that turned out to be good?"

"Both."

Bummer. I was really hoping to avoid telling them another rare but ridiculous story about one of my Lighthouse colleagues. So I gave them one of my own.

"Okay, let's do the dumb one first. I was recently facilitating an off-site meeting for one of my technology clients. They were explaining that they were having a hard time managing new sales leads, so I suggested that they go out and get some better software tools for lead management."

"Why was that a dumb idea?" Janet wondered.

"Because one of their products, albeit a minor one, is a lead management software suite."

Their winces suggested that they felt sorry for me. I gladly accepted their pity.

"How did you survive that one?" the Penguin wondered.

"The same way you survive them all. You admit that it was dumb. In fact, you celebrate it."

I went to the board and added,

Celebrate your mistakes.

"How do you do that?"

"You admit it was a bad idea as soon as you realize it. You laugh at yourself. You take their ribbing. And most important, you don't stop making suggestions. Most of your ideas won't be horrible. Even the ones that aren't so good won't hurt you as long as you're humble enough to acknowledge that you're not an expert. And if you've built trust with the client, they don't think about it for a second."

"How do you know?"

165

"Because every time I hear someone make a dumb suggestion, the client just says 'No, that wouldn't work,' and they move on. It's really not that big of a deal."

"But what if most of your ideas are bad ones?" It was Kendrick.

"Well, then you've got a big problem. But it's not because you're too naked or vulnerable. It's because you're not competent."

They laughed.

"The idea is that your clients are looking for good suggestions, and they don't mind sifting through some not-so-good ones as long as they're offered with good intentions and with no ego attached."

"Okay, give me some dumb suggestions that turned out to be good ones." Kendrick was pushing me along, but seemingly with enthusiasm.

So I told them about Amy's suggestion to the medical technology company about licensing from a competitor. And about her idea to create a family-friendly, alcohol-free section at 49er games. And Dick's recommendation that one of his manufacturing clients move all their factories to the U.S. and go with a made-in-the-USA marketing plan. And whether the people sitting in the room thought those ideas were good ones didn't really matter, because, as I reminded them, the clients ended up implementing the suggestions, and, more important still, they worked.

I was starting to feel extremely confident that the people in the room were eating out of my hand now, and that the final part of my little lecture would be relatively easy. And then Marty walked into the room.

DECEPTION

arty went straight to Jim Kendrick. The fact that he didn't even look at me or acknowledge that I was in the middle of a presentation was infuriating.

Marty whispered something in Kendrick's ear and then, for the first time, glanced at me while trying to hide the smile on his face. And before I knew what was happening, he turned and left the room.

Jim Kendrick stood and went to the middle of the conference table near the speaker phone.

"Gentlemen, I guess you've heard enough. Is there anything else you need from us right now?"

At first, I thought he was talking to the partners sitting around the table. But his voice had that tone people use when they're talking to someone on speakerphone. And others in the room didn't seem confused, but were staring at the triangular phone sitting in front of them.

Finally, after a few seconds' delay, a voice came over the phone.

"No, I'm good. We'll finalize the details on Monday. Thanks, everyone."

Jim then addressed someone else on the line. "What about you, Michael? What did you think?"

"I thought he nailed it, probably better than I could have. Great job, Jack."

I said "Thank you" half-heartedly, not knowing who I was talking to and why there were people on the line.

Jim ended the phone conversation. "Thanks guys. We'll talk soon." And he hit a button on the phone and hung up.

At first I didn't know what to say. I looked at Jim, but he was shaking hands with the Penguin.

"Excuse me," I said, not delicately. "Do you mind telling me what's going on here?"

FURTHER
EXPLANATION

Jim turned toward me, smiling in a way that suggested both pride and guilt. "Yes, of course. I owe you an explanation, Jack."

He went back to his chair. "The two gentlemen on the phone were Tom Paulson from Strategic Insights, and Michael Casey, the founder of Lighthouse. I thought they should hear today's meeting."

Before I could ask for more context, he finished.

"See, we're selling Lighthouse to Strategic Insights, and I wanted Michael to confirm that your description of his company was accurate, and I wanted Tom Paulson to hear it directly from someone with no vested interest in selling the firm. He and Paulson were listening from the beginning, and discussing your presentation on another line. Evidently, Paulson liked what he heard, and Michael affirmed that it was true, and so we have a deal."

I was at a loss for words, but apparently my face betrayed my anger. Janet tried to preempt any tirade I was considering.

"Jack, it was the best thing to do."

"You mean letting them secretly listen to my presentation, or selling the company?"

"Well, selling the company is what I was thinking about."

I was obviously dumbfounded, and pretty pissed off, so Kendrick continued.

"Here's the deal. Not long after we purchased Lighthouse, Marty started to worry that the cultural differences were bigger than he had thought. He was getting nervous about how it would all turn out, that it would fall back on him, and decided we should cut our losses before we screwed this thing up even more."

I shouldn't have been surprised that Marty was behind all this.

Kendrick continued, "Over time, I started to agree with him. As much as I liked their profitability numbers, I talked to a few people in the industry and realized that our consultants are just a different breed from theirs. I even called Paulson at Strategic Insights a few weeks ago and floated the idea by him."

"A few weeks ago? You knew that the merger wasn't going to work then?"

"No. In fact, I wasn't convinced of that completely until your presentation today. I mean, there's no doubt in my mind that we wouldn't be able to do this naked, vulnerable stuff. It's an 'old dog trying to learn new tricks' kind of thing."

"So when did you set up today's call?"

"Last night, after you left. It was all contingent on hearing your presentation and having Michael Casey verify what we suspected."

"Why didn't you tell me?"

"Because I didn't want you to be distracted by what we were trying to do. You were passionate last night, and I wanted you to be passionate today."

I was having a hard time digesting it all, trying to decide whether to empathize with Kendrick or loathe him.

He then pulled a classic Kendrick. "Well, I'm late for another meeting." He looked at me. "You can talk to Marty about how all this plays out for you."

And he turned to leave.

"What about the third fear?" I asked, sounding pathetic, I'm sure.

Barely turning around to address me, he responded, "Sorry, I'm late. And the sale is pretty much a done deal. Thanks, Jack." And he was gone, followed quickly by Finley, Larry, and DeWitt.

I felt like a little boy who didn't get picked on a kickball team at recess.

Janet, the Penguin, and two others remained seated. The look on Janet's face suggested she might actually be restraining some sort of emotion, and after an awkward silence, she spoke. "Well, I want to hear about the last fear."

The Penguin and the others nodded.

Now, if I had sensed any pity from them, I'd have politely but insistently refused. But they seemed genuinely curious—maybe even a little desperate—to know the rest of the model.

Setting aside my frustration, not to mention the uncertainty I was feeling about what I was going to do with my career, I decided that I would finish my presentation—after a quick break so I could pull myself together a little.

THE THIRD FEAR

uring the break I called Diane and gave her the forty-two-second version of what had just happened. I had never heard so many PG-13 words come out of her mouth. When I went back to the conference room, I half expected no one to be there. But there they sat. Trying to be somewhat cool, I dove in.

"Okay, the third and final fear that the Lighthouse consultants seem to have overcome is the fear of feeling inferior to their clients."

I forced myself to go to the whiteboard and write it down with my favorite blue pen.

#3 Fear of feeling inferior

I was not surprised to see that my smaller audience seemed more confused by this one than the others, so I explained.

"One of the last things consultants want is for their clients to look down on them or, even worse, look right through them. There is something about wanting them to see you as being important that goes with the job."

The Penguin frowned. "This sounds like the last one, the fear of looking stupid."

I nodded. "Yeah, it does. And they're related, I suppose. But different. The fear of being embarrassed or looking stupid is about taking an intellectual risk. It's about the pride of not wanting to be wrong. The fear of feeling inferior is more about humility as a person, not needing to be the center of attention. Even taking on a role of true subservience to a client."

My students were a little clearer, but still not quite where I wanted them. The woman who headed up the organizational practice—I'm pretty sure her name was Helen—made a helpful suggestion. "What are some of the principles that go with this one?"

"Great idea." I turned toward the whiteboard and decided to write down all four principles at once. "Let's see."

> Take a bullet for the client.
> Make everything about the client.
> Honor the client's work.
> Do the dirty work.

I decided not to wait for them to object, but instead beat them to the punch. "Yes, I know that these sound like a consultant's version of the Boy Scout oath. But there's more to them than that."

Janet raised her hand. "I think it also sounds like the butt-kisser's oath."

Everyone laughed, especially hearing that come from Janet. And because it wasn't offered as a criticism or an attack, I enjoyed the moment as much as anyone.

"Right," I said, "if you do this in an obsequious kind of way, then that's what it will be. But remember, you're the same consultant who is telling them the kind truth and entering the danger, so they're not going to see you as telling them what they want to hear. That's what makes this so powerful."

I could see little imaginary lightbulbs starting to flicker over the heads of my audience, so I pressed on.

"There is something so powerful about a person who in one moment can be confident enough to confront a client about a sensitive personal issue, and then in the next moment humble themselves and take a position of servitude. It's the paradoxical nature of it all that makes it work."

The Penguin laughed, but not cynically. "Now you're sounding like a professor. How about a few specific examples?"

I gladly obliged and decided to start with "taking a bullet" because it was the most difficult.

I began by telling them the story of Michael Casey being skewered by the executives at the strategy session. And if I do say so myself, I did a good job of helping them understand why that story was an example of courage and strength, and not weakness.

"So you're not saying that you should let clients abuse you." Janet asked her question in the form of a statement, like the opposite of *Jeopardy*.

"No. It's about knowing that in certain moments you have to offer yourself up as a minor sacrifice to help them accomplish what they need to accomplish. Letting them abuse you, on the other hand, would be a terrible disservice. I know it seems like a fine line, but it's a real one, and it can be done."

174

"Give me another example," Janet asked. "Maybe a little less dramatic."

I thought about it. "Okay, you're helping a client implement a new program and it's not working. They're taking heat for it from employees, and you're not sure what the problem is. You stand there in front of whoever is listening and tell them that you've obviously overlooked something, that this is your responsibility to figure it out, and that you apologize for the frustration and inconvenience."

"That's harder than it sounds," Helen remarked.

"Yes it is," I assured her. "It is painful. And it is powerful."

Suddenly the Penguin had an epiphany. "Hey, this sounds like the fear of losing the business now."

I agreed. "Yes, sometimes there is overlap. If your biggest fear is losing the business, that's one thing. But if your fear is standing there and having to absorb the blame for something that may not be entirely your fault, that's about being comfortable with temporary inferiority. In most cases, it's a little bit of both."

He acknowledged that my answer wasn't ridiculous.

Janet looked at her watch. "What about 'Honor the client's work'?"

I tried to go fast. "That's about genuinely displaying enthusiasm and respect for what the client does."

"What if you're not enthusiastic about what the client does?" the Penguin asked.

"You find a way to get enthusiastic. I mean, if you're trying to help a client do a better job of manufacturing paper clips, then you need to realize that it's important to them, their clients, their vendors, and their families, and that paper clips are their bread and butter. If you can't get excited about helping them—not about paper clips necessarily, but about your client's livelihood—then by all means let another consultant work with them. You owe them that much."

"What if they do something that you think is just plain bad?" he countered.

"For instance?"

"I don't know. Pornography. Tobacco. That kind of thing."

I smiled. "Well, I don't know about you, but I'm not going to take a client that does something I find morally indefensible."

"But the examples are not always that cut and dried."

"You're right. Last month an on-line gambling company in Vancouver called Lighthouse about working with them. We talked about it and agreed it wasn't something that we would feel good about promoting and that we couldn't honor the client's business. So we called the client and told them exactly that."

"What exactly is dirty work?" Janet asked, pushing hard to get through all the points.

"Lots of things. Sometimes it's typing up notes after a meeting, sometimes it's going out to get food. Other times it's cranking out slides for them for a meeting."

"So, naked consultants always do that stuff?" Janet wasn't liking this part, I could tell.

"No, but they make it very clear that they'll do their share of it, and more, and they're not above anything when it comes to helping the clients."

Janet accepted my explanation.

Helen didn't. "I still don't understand how this is different from not wanting to look stupid. Or why you make a distinction."

I knew there was a difference, but I was having a hard time thinking about how to describe it. And then an idea occurred to me. "Let's try something that might help with this. Everyone here look at the three fears and tell me which your biggest challenge is."

They looked at me like I had asked them to strip down to their skivvies and do the funky chicken.

"Come on," I urged them, "you have to have some idea which of these is hardest for you."

My audience members were now studying the board and glancing around the room as though they were comparing themselves to one another. Finally, the Penguin spoke.

"I don't like to look dumb." He said it emphatically. "Not knowing the answer and getting something wrong kills me." He then explained that this made sense given his Myers-Briggs personality type, something having to do with being a rational person. I could relate to that.

Helen countered, "I don't care so much about that one. My big thing is keeping the client happy and not having them reject me. I guess that's about losing the business."

I nodded my agreement with her analysis.

"That's probably because I'm a pleaser, and I'm really competitive. The idea that someone beats me, and that a client or prospect didn't think I was good enough to earn or keep their business, worries me the most."

177

The Penguin smiled. "Not me. If they reject me, I figure they were just too dumb to understand how I could help them."

We laughed.

"I'm serious. That's what my wife calls my arrogance thing."

Now Janet was staring at the board and nodding her head. "Okay. I think I get this now. One of my staff members has the inferiority one. It's a pride thing. Whenever a client asks her to do something that she thinks is below her education level, or if they don't appreciate her enough, she gets all bent out of shape. I've always thought she lacked humility, and so this makes sense."

"What's yours?" I asked Janet.

"I was afraid you were going to ask me that." She looked at the board again.

"What do you guys think?" She asked Helen and the Penguin and the remaining partner in the room, a nameless, faceless man about whom I remember nothing.

In unison, they replied, "Losing the business."

She smiled. "Yeah, yeah. You're right."

Suddenly her expression changed: she looked puzzled.

"What's up?" I asked her, feeling very comfortable with this particular group of students.

She studied the board, apparently still working out her thoughts. "I was just thinking about my husband's business. He's a residential contractor, a home builder. His clients love him, and almost all of his business comes from unsolicited referrals." She paused. "I think he does most of these things. I mean, he's never described it like this and I don't think he has a specific methodology around any of it, but I think he's definitely very naked with his clients."

The others chuckled.

And then I saw a lightbulb go on over Helen's head. She asked her colleagues a question. "Which department within the firm provides the best internal service?"

After two quick seconds, Janet and the Penguin and the faceless man said almost in unison, "Legal."

"And why is that?" asked Helen.

The Penguin answered without hesitation. "Because Jeremy ... " He paused and turned to me to explain: "He's our corporate counsel—and he does most of this stuff too."

Janet was nodding her head. "They admit when they're wrong. They tell us when they don't know something. They roll up their sleeves and do the dirty work that other legal departments think is beneath them."

Helen smiled. "And they definitely tell us the kind truth."

Her colleagues laughed, apparently referring to a situation that I wasn't privy to.

It was at that happy moment that Marty poked his head into the conference room and interrupted. "Jack, can you stop by my office when you're done here? I'll be there for another hour or so."

I nodded, and he left, having severely diminished the levity in the windowless room, which was suddenly quiet.

The Penguin broke the silence. "So what do you think, Jack?"

"I think that you're right about the legal department. Whenever I deal with one of their—"

He interrupted me. "No. I mean, what do you think about the conversation you're about to have with Marty?"

I was surprised, both by the question and by his concern.

I thought about if for a second. "Maybe I should ask you. You probably have a better idea."

He smiled in a kindly, patronizing way. "I wish I did. But as you know, Kendrick pretty much lets us run our departments the way we want. It's probably up to Marty."

"That's not the answer I was looking for."

The smiles on the faces in the room seemed to be a mixture of pity and affection. I accepted them both.

"So, do you guys have any other questions about the Lighthouse approach?"

They shook their heads and definitely seemed more concerned about my career than about satisfying their curiosity.

I pushed them a little. "Do you think that Kendrick and Black can use this?"

"Are you kidding?" It was Helen. "We'd be crazy not to."

"I'm not sure everyone here could put it into practice, though." I think it was the nameless, faceless guy who said it, but for some reason, I still can't recall a single thing about him.

Helen agreed with him. "No doubt. There are certain people in the firm who would have a very hard time being naked. And more important, would have no interest in nakedness."

We laughed. And then Janet said something that again made me want to stand on my tippy toes and kiss her.

"But I'm going to do what I can to teach my people."

The Penguin seemed to be encouraged by his colleague's declaration. "Me too. Why wouldn't we?"

At that moment one of the receptionists from the front desk, a new woman who had evidently joined the firm since I had moved down to Half Moon Bay, came into the room. "Excuse me. Is Jack Bauer here?"

I raised my hand.

"Marty's getting anxious and is wondering what time you think you'll be stopping by his office."

I looked at my room full of new friends.

Janet said what they were all thinking. "You better go."

I agreed, and began what felt like a death march.

DROPPING SHOES

As I approached Darth Vader's office, I tried to keep myself in "naked mode." But I can't deny that I was fighting fear, not so much because of *what* might happen, but because of *how* it would happen. To have to stand there and take Marty's crap was more than I was ready for, especially after the afternoon I had just had.

I said a prayer for strength.

When I opened the door, Marty was on the phone, so I paused in the doorway. He smiled falsely and pointed to a chair in front of his desk. I remained standing just to defy him.

After a moment he wrapped up the conversation and finally spoke to me.

"Crazy times, huh?" he said with a smile.

"If by crazy you mean having to deal with a self-absorbed boss who will throw you to the wolves at the first sign of trouble, then yes, these times are indeed crazy." And yes, I actually said that, but with a smile. I wish I had been able to muster more self-control, but I wasn't.

"Whoa. Whoa. Hold on. I think you should give me a chance to explain."

The better part of me won out. "Okay. I'm sorry. I'm listening."

Marty paused, as though he really didn't have anything to say in his defense, and that his request to plead his case was simply a ruse. But being the slick guy that he was, he found something to say. "This hasn't been easy for me either. I had no idea how strange the culture at Lighthouse was going to be, and that we wouldn't be able to make this thing work."

He paused to see if I would empathize with him. When it was clear that I wouldn't, he continued, "And I was under a little pressure myself to get us out of the situation. Putting together this deal with Strategic Insights wasn't easy or pretty."

I decided that remaining silent was best, both to ensure that I wouldn't say anything I would regret and to make him stew a little.

And then Marty did something that I could not have anticipated. "Look, Jack, I'm sorry. I know I've been an ass. None of this turned out the way I hoped it would, and you got caught right in the middle of it. And I didn't do much to get you out of it. I don't know what to say."

There it was again. Someone that I was determined to hate—or, with a nod to Sister Rose Marie, dislike—doing something redemptive. How dare this guy who had caused me so many problems suddenly force me to have to grow, again!

I took a breath. "Well, I appreciate the apology." I was at a loss. "I do."

There was a moment of silence, until Marty moved the conversation forward.

"Anyway, as you know, I'm going to retire next summer, and we're going to find a partner to run this division. I've already talked to Kendrick about it, and we agreed it should be you."

Four months ago, even four weeks ago, I would have been relieved, if not slightly ecstatic, to hear those words. Today I was decidedly ambivalent. Or maybe even disappointed.

"Okay." That was all I could say. I could tell Marty was hoping for more enthusiasm and gratitude, but I just couldn't muster it.

"Is this something you're interested in doing?" he asked. "You don't seem quite as excited as I expected."

I tried to recover. "No, it's just, yes, I'm interested. I'm just tired, and this has been a crazy day, and everything is coming at me kind of fast."

"I can only imagine," he said, and moved on to the topic of next steps. "So, take the next day or two to wrap things up down at Lighthouse and get set up here again. In fact, take a day off in the mean time. I know it's been a lot of work lately."

I nodded my head, not knowing what to say. Finally I managed an "Okay, thanks." And walked out.

GUT CHECK

By the time I finished telling Diane the longer version of the story, I was a little tired of having her say "No, no, no. Tell me exactly what they said." But I couldn't blame her, and I obliged her as well as I could.

"Wow," she declared when I was done. "I wish I could have been there."

We both agreed that she would have strangled Marty, and that her presence would not have been to my advantage.

I spent the rest of the evening with the family, avoiding any more discussion of work. And again, I spent more time thinking than sleeping that night.

The next morning I went to Half Moon Bay to tell Luck, Amy, and Matt what had happened and to clear out my desk there. During my drive to the coast, the reality of the situation really hit me.

First, it would be the last time I make this drive, or work with these people. Though it had been only a few months, I couldn't deny how much I had come to enjoy Lighthouse, and how much it had changed me.

Second, I didn't know how we were going to deal with the clients I had been working with. Transitioning to a new consultant usually took weeks, and I didn't have that kind of time.

My colleagues' reaction to my narrative from the previous two days at Kendrick and Black surprised me. I expected them to be somewhat indifferent, or maybe even relieved, about the sale to Strategic Insights. They weren't. When I asked why, I was stunned by Dick's response.

"Because of you," he replied, as though I should have known.

True to form, Matt was sarcastic, or so I thought. "Do you know how hard it's been breaking you in? I don't think I have it in me to go through that again."

We laughed, and we talked about what we should do with my clients. And then it hit me. There was no way I could go back to work at K&B after my experience of the past four months. And so I laid my cards on the table.

"Do you think I should try to jump over to Strategic Insights and keep working here?"

None of my friends looked at all surprised by my question. In fact, it seemed that they had been waiting for me to ask it. But their response blew me away.

"Not unless you want to work alone."

I was completely confused. They didn't wait for me to ask the obvious questions.

Amy made the announcement. "We're leaving."

"What?"

Dick confirmed it. "We're giving them six months to integrate things and transition the clients to new consultants, and then we're leaving."

"Why?"

Matt responded first. "I just told you. We don't want to have to break in another new guy."

They laughed.

Dick clarified the situation for me. "Look, part of what Matt said is right. But more than anything, this is just the right time to make a change. I'm going to semi-retire and cut back on my hours."

"Me too," Amy announced. "My kids are at an age that I want to spend more time at home."

"Yeah," Matt complained. "I'm the one being abandoned here." He laughed.

"What are you going to do?" I asked him.

"I'm going to start my own practice. Focus more on organizational stuff."

"So where does that leave me?" I wanted to know.

"You're pretty much screwed," Matt teased.

I laughed, but in that way a man laughs when, if he were a boy, he might have cried.

ONWARD

When I turned down the offer to run the strategy practice at Kendrick and Black, Marty had the gall to suggest I was ungrateful. If it were a movie, I might have punched him in the face. But that is neither realistic nor noble, so I merely smiled and said, "Wow."

Two hours later I received an offer from Tom Paulson, the managing partner at Strategic Insights, to run the practice formerly known as Lighthouse. Even before I hung up the phone, I decided that I should turn down that offer too. I'd had enough of institutional consulting, and besides, Matt had suggested that I join him in starting his consulting practice. Suddenly that was sounding like the best option.

But I couldn't quite decline the offer right away. That's because Tom Paulson, who had sounded like a decent enough guy during my two brief phone conversations with him, asked me to come to Half Moon Bay to give him an opportunity to change my mind. I decided that refusing really would be a sign of ingratitude, so I agreed.

When I discussed all of this with Diane that night, I was surprised by her opinion, or lack thereof. Normally, she would have showered me with more advice than I might have asked for, but now she was holding back and simply reassuring me that I would make the right decision.

"Whatever you decide, just make sure you can be yourself and enjoy what you're doing."

"Thanks for nothing," I teased her, hoping she would make my decision easier. She just smiled.

When I arrived at Lighthouse the next day, I strolled a little more slowly along the corridor, stopping to take a long drink from the little fountain between the boys' and girls' bathrooms. I was even a little disappointed that I didn't have to pee, because I would have liked to use the little urinals there one last time.

When I entered the conference room, I saw only two men, neither of whom I knew, though one looked vaguely familiar. They introduced themselves.

"Hi Jack, I'm Tom Paulson." He was a nicely dressed, professional-looking man, the kind you would think would run a high-end consulting firm. And from the smile on his face and everything else I could gather about him in that nanosecond, he did indeed look like a decent guy.

The other man, the one who looked just slightly familiar to me, was older but wore jeans and a polo shirt. He smiled at me as though he knew me or, better yet, was somehow proud of me. It was strange.

"I'm Michael Casey. I've heard a lot about you, Jack."

Though I suppose I shouldn't have been completely surprised, I can't deny that I was stunned to finally be standing face to face with the man who for a number of years had provoked my jealousy and anger—and now, somehow, my admiration.

189

Michael looked familiar because I had seen informal pictures of him around the office. But his voice I had heard only once, two days earlier on the speakerphone.

"I want to thank you for doing such a nice job explaining my firm the other day."

I nodded, accepting his compliment but not knowing what to say.

Fortunately, he continued. "And I don't know why I never thought about your model. The three fears."

"Probably because you never had to."

He smiled. "I suppose so."

We sat down, and I asked about his daughter, wife, and grandchildren. He thanked me for my concern—he seemed to genuinely appreciate it—and reported that they were "still struggling but hanging in there."

Then he changed the subject. "Jack, I'm here to ask you to stay on and run this office."

I turned to Tom Paulson, who smiled and made his pitch. "We want to maintain this culture and see if we can't infect the rest of our firm with it."

Michael continued, "I can't blame Dick and Amy for wanting to leave. They're in a place in their lives where it makes sense to move on. But I'm pretty sure we could talk Matt into staying, as long as there's a leader here for him to work with."

I didn't say anything, but my body language must have suggested that I wasn't convinced yet, because Michael went on.

"Listen, I don't want to see this place disintegrate, and I don't want to see people over here lose their jobs. When I left, I knew that it might not be perfect and that there was a possibility things would unravel, but when I heard you on the phone this week, I decided that there was a chance to keep it going. And that's why I got on a plane for the first time in months."

I couldn't help but feel for this man who had seen his life turned upside down. And I was genuinely surprised at what Tom Paulson had said, and how sincere he seemed. I didn't want to be rash, but neither did I want to leave these decent men hanging.

"Well, I need to talk to my wife," I said, knowing she would be happy for me, "and if I can talk Matt into—"

Michael interrupted me, sheepishly. "Actually, I already did."

"You did what?"

"I asked Matt if he would stay if you agreed to run the practice, and he said yes. I'm sorry I didn't wait, but I wanted to—"

Now I interrupted him. "No. That's fine. I understand."

Suddenly the surreal nature of the moment hit me. In a matter of days, I had gone from anticipating being fired and having my career ruined, to being offered the job I thought I had wanted, to refusing that job and being called ungrateful, to being courted by this pseudo-mythical figure sitting in front of me in blue jeans.

"Wait a second," I said, catching myself. "I already know what my wife is going to say. Of course I'll take the job."

Tom shook my hand enthusiastically, which was nice. Michael just smiled at me like a parent who had known all along what I was going to do.

After we called Matt to let him know what had happened, I called Diane to tell her the news. Her reaction confirmed that I had made the right decision.

So I thanked Tom Paulson and made arrangements to meet with him two days later to finalize the agreement. I said goodbye to Michael Casey, whom I would not see again.

As I left the building, I could not deny that I felt better about my career than I had in a long time. Maybe ever. And as painful as the last few months had been, I knew that it was something to be grateful for. I even considered sending Marty a thank-you note, but decided against it.

As I walked down the breezeway and passed the boys' and girls' bathrooms and child-sized drinking fountains, I couldn't help but think of Sister Rose Marie. I decided I would send her a thank-you note instead.

The Model

THE ORIGINS OF
GETTING NAKED

I n the late 1990s, I helped start a management consulting firm called The Table Group that provides a variety of services to a wide range of clients in just about every respectable industry imaginable. From the beginning we adopted a simple and informal approach to serving clients that provoked surprising levels of loyalty and trust. This book is about that approach, which we call naked consulting.

Explaining the effectiveness of our naked consulting and service model is something of a challenge for me because, unlike in my other books, it requires me to cite my own firm as an example. The possibility that this will come across in any way as immodest is particularly terrifying for me because one of the keys to the naked service model—as well as the basis for the core values of our firm—is humility. But if I don't adequately convey the power of our approach, perhaps you won't think it is worth adopting. And I definitely think it's worth adopting. So here goes.

Naked service has allowed us to build extraordinary trust among our clients over the years, beyond anything we could have imagined. They have welcomed us into their most critical and sensitive discussions without hesitation. They have consistently sought our advice and counsel, often about matters that were outside of the scope of the core services we provided. They have kept us around even when budgets were tight. And they have vouched for us enthusiastically and authentically with other clients who were considering working with us.

In essence, our clients have treated us more like real partners and team members than as vendors or outsiders. Or as we like to say, they treat us like members of their family. Cousins, maybe, but really close ones. And aside from making our work more enjoyable, profitable, and rewarding than we would have thought possible, this naked approach to consulting has allowed us to more effectively serve and help those clients in meaningful ways.

Now, the story in this book is about a management consulting firm, because that is what we are. However, the naked approach is certainly not limited to our field. It applies to anyone who provides ongoing, relationship-based advice, counsel, or expertise to a customer, inside or outside of a company. Or better yet, it applies to anyone whose success is tied to building loyal and sticky relationships with the people they serve.

Okay, let's look at what naked service entails.

NAKED SERVICE
DEFINED

At its core, naked service boils down to the ability of a service provider to be vulnerable—to embrace uncommon levels of humility, selflessness, and transparency for the good of a client.

As obvious as that may sound, it is more difficult than it seems, because humility and selflessness and transparency often entail suffering. And suffering is not something most human beings, especially in our modern culture, understand or welcome. Most of us live our lives trying to avoid awkward and painful situations, which is why it is no surprise that we are susceptible to the three fears that prevent us from building trust and loyalty with our clients.

#1: FEAR OF LOSING THE BUSINESS

No service provider wants to lose clients, business opportunities, or revenue. Ironically, though, this fear of losing the business actually hurts our ability to keep and increase business, because it causes us to avoid doing the difficult things that engender greater loyalty and trust with the people we're trying to serve.

What clients want more than anything is to know that we're more interested in helping them than we are in maintaining our revenue source. And when we do something, or fail to do something, in order to protect our business, they eventually lose respect for us and understandably question whether they should trust us.

Naked service providers refuse to be overly concerned about the possibility of losing a client or, for that matter, being undercompensated or having their ideas misappropriated by a client. In fact, they willingly put themselves in positions of exposure in each of these areas, knowing that by doing so they will earn the trust of their clients. They understand that in the end, more goodwill comes about even if there are setbacks along the way.

It's worth reminding ourselves that clients can smell fear and are repelled by it. They are attracted to a service provider who will be honest and direct with them, even if it might jeopardize the relationship. If I remember correctly, the same principles applied in dating: girls prefer honest and self-assured guys over desperate ones who tell them what they want to hear. Sounds crazy and counterintuitive, I know, but it is true.

#2: FEAR OF BEING EMBARRASSED

No one likes making mistakes in public and having to endure the scrutiny of spectators, especially when those spectators are paying us for our advice or counsel. And yet, like a fifth-grader, we know that the only thing worse than raising our hand and having the wrong answer is failing to put our hand up at all (and realizing that more often than not, we did indeed have the right answer). This fear, then, is rooted in pride, and it is ultimately about avoiding the appearance of ignorance, wanting to be seen instead as smart or competent.

Naked service providers are so concerned about helping a client that they are willing to ask questions and make suggestions even if those questions and suggestions could turn out to be laughably wrong. They readily admit what they don't know and are quick to point out—even to celebrate—their errors because protecting their intellectual ego is not important to them.

Clients come to trust naked service providers because they know that they will not hold back their ideas, hide their mistakes, or edit themselves in order to save face. As painful as this can be for a consultant who wants to be seen as smart, it is a turnoff to clients who want to hear all of our suggestions, and who are yearning for transparency and modesty—qualities that are immensely more attractive than intelligence.

#3: FEAR OF FEELING INFERIOR

Like the previous fear, this one has its roots in ego, but there is an important difference between the two. Fear of feeling inferior is not about our intellectual pride, but rather about preserving our sense of importance and social standing relative to a client.

It is completely natural for service providers to yearn for respect and admiration, and to have a disdain for being overlooked, condescended to, or treated as though we are inferior. And so it is no surprise that, as consultants, we try to achieve and preserve a certain level of standing and importance in the eyes of our clients. But sometimes we forget that the word "service" shares the same root meaning as "servant" and even "subservience."

Naked service providers not only overcome their need to feel important in the eyes of their clients, but also purposefully put themselves in a lower position. They do whatever a client needs them to do to help them improve, even if that calls for the service provider to be overlooked or temporarily looked down on. Ironically, clients come to trust and respect service providers who do this and ultimately come to think more highly of them. That's because there is nothing more attractive and admirable than people who willingly and cheerfully set their egos aside and make the needs of others more important than their own.

SHEDDING THE
THREE FEARS

Vulnerable service providers demonstrate nakedness by engaging in a variety of simple but powerful practices, all of which correspond to one or more of the three primary fears. And as important as it is to understand the fears that underlie these principles, the specific actions that demonstrate naked service are what is required to achieve client loyalty.

The principles of naked services are as follows.

ALWAYS CONSULT INSTEAD OF SELL
(Fear of Losing the Business)

Naked service providers transform every sales situation into an opportunity to demonstrate the value of what they do. They avoid, as much as possible, telling clients what they would do if they were to be hired; instead, they just start serving them as though they were already a client. And they don't worry about whether the potential client will take advantage of their generosity; they know that for every client that does, nine others will appreciate their generosity and start to see themselves as a client even before they formally decide to become one.

Sales situations then become service giveaways, which are more enjoyable experiences because they give the service provider higher levels of confidence than they would have had if they were simply trying to convince a potential client to make a decision.

Many of the people who work with me would probably say that I'm a good salesperson, but the fact is, I'm miserable at traditional sales. I don't like to talk about fees, and I don't like to go for "the close." But I love consulting, so I just go into sales meetings with the idea that I'm going to find a way to help them in some meaningful way. Then, if they choose not to hire me, I realize it was probably the right decision because they could see exactly what it is I do and decide whether or not it is something they need.

GIVE AWAY THE BUSINESS
(Fear of Losing the Business)

This principle has two applications. On the one hand, it is related to the "always consult instead of sell" principle because it is about giving a prospective client advice and service even before they agree to become a paying client. By demonstrating generosity and trust, you drastically increase the likelihood of making them a client, not to mention proving to them that you can help them.

The other part of giving away the business is more financial. It entails always erring on the side of the client when it comes to fees. Because you're interested in a long-term relationship with a client, it is in your best interest to show them that you are more focused on helping them than you are in maximizing your short-term revenue.

A colleague of mine once did work for an ongoing client without having agreed to a price ahead of time. When he sent a bill for his services, the client responded with a genuine "Whoa, I didn't think it was going to cost that much." Instead of pressing for the full amount, my co-worker simply charged them what they expected the work would cost. That client continues to work with our firm today.

Another consultant I know who practices naked service met with a potential client who admitted that they were hoping to do the work themselves instead of hiring an outsider. He met with them and gave them the information and advice they needed to do it without him. Two years later, they came back to him to be a paying client, remembering that he had been more interested in helping them than in charging them.

TELL THE KIND TRUTH
(Fear of Losing the Business)

Naked service providers will confront a client with a difficult message, even when the client might not like hearing it. As a result, they put the relationship with the client at risk, knowing that it is more important to serve the client's needs than it is to protect the service provider's own business.

But they do this in a way that recognizes the dignity and humanity of the client. Instead of bluntly hitting them over the head with a difficult message, they present their counsel with kindness, empathy, and respect. Still, they don't sugarcoat their advice or present it in an obsequious way. Naked consultants understand that they have a responsibility for being a truth teller, even if this means they will be sacrificed.

A consultant I know was working for a client, a native New Yorker, who was having trouble working with his

Southern colleagues. He was being too direct—an approach that had served him well in his career back home but was now intimidating his Southern peers. The consultant knew he needed to address the client, but in a way he could hear. Drawing on characters from the movie *The Godfather*, he said, "Maybe you could be a little less like Sonny and a little more like Michael." The client immediately understood, agreed, and over time was able to change his style. On numerous occasions since then, he has expressed his gratitude for the advice and the way it was delivered.

ENTER THE DANGER
(Fear of Losing the Business)

Naked service providers don't shy away from uncomfortable situations; they step right into the middle of them. This concept is taken from the world of improvisational theater.

In improv, it is natural for novices to avoid playing off of a bizarre comment or behavior of a fellow actor, worried that they won't know how to build on it. Great improv actors take the opposite approach by seeking out and engaging in the most wacky situations (entering the danger), knowing that this is where an opportunity for genius lies.

When it comes to consulting and service, entering the danger has to do with having the courage to fearlessly deal with an issue that everyone else is afraid to address. Perhaps more than any other service a consultant provides, this one provokes the most appreciation from clients, many of whom have grown weary of avoiding the "elephant in the room"—one that, over time, has become smellier and messier and therefore more untouchable.

204

When a naked service provider stops and says, "Hey, does anyone else smell that?" the consultant usually becomes a hero. Clients come to see them as having courage and integrity—qualities that are disarming, attractive, and often rare. And so "dangerous" situations become opportunities for adding value and building trust.

This tactic can look similar to telling the kind truth, but it is different because it is done in a group setting in the midst of a potentially difficult moment. A friend of mine was working with a senior executive who went off on a typical, somewhat abusive tirade in front of his team. When he finished, the room went silent and, as usual, everyone just waited for the moment to pass. My friend didn't let that happen, but instead said, "Okay, I think it would be a good idea to talk about the impact that these situations have on the team." For the first time, they discussed it and were able to help the executive admit what he needed to work on and how it could help the team.

I once worked with the leadership team of a software company, a group of extremely intelligent and driven people. After watching them struggle with the issue of lead generation and marketing, I sensed that others in the room shared my confusion about the company's basic customer promise. I spoke up and said, "I'm sorry, but I just don't understand your value proposition. Am I the only one, or is this confusing to you guys too?" At first, a few of the executives looked at me like I was a moron. Just as I was ready to admit my mistake, the head of customer service said, "I don't get it either," followed by a handful of other key executives who admitted their confusion too. This was an example of two principles

205

of naked consulting—entering the danger and asking dumb questions, which I'll describe next.

ASK DUMB QUESTIONS
(Fear of Being Embarrassed)

Naked service providers are the ones who ask the questions that others in the room are afraid to ask out of fear that they would embarrass themselves. They realize that if they ask five questions and three of them could be considered "dumb," the potential benefit that comes from the other two makes it worthwhile.

Most of us wouldn't think a 40-percent hit rate would justify the potential humiliation of being perceived as unprepared or intellectually deficient. But clients love it. They're almost always going to remember the great question we asked and forget about the others, especially when we can quickly and humbly acknowledge the questions that turn out to be poor.

Think about the times you've been in a room and had a question that you thought might be too obvious to ask. And then someone else asks it, and you look at them with a sense of gratitude and respect. That's how clients see us, if we have the courage to ask.

Once I was in a relatively tedious meeting with an executive team that was reviewing their budget for the year. As I looked over the spreadsheet that they were reviewing, I noticed that in the marketing area there was no line item for advertising. Because the company had just gone public, it seemed strange that they wouldn't be doing any advertising, so I raised my hand and asked about it. A new colleague of mine who was also in the room at the time later told me that he was mortified by my question. He thought to himself, "Come on, of course these people thought about advertising. It's probably just buried within one of the other marketing categories."

He was as surprised as I was when the CEO responded to my question by turning to the marketing VP for an answer. The head of marketing looked a little stunned and said "Well, I wasn't sure if you wanted us to do any advertising this year ... " And so they clarified the situation and moved funds into that part of the budget. The executive team thanked me for helping them see something they had missed. Still, I had been completely prepared for them to say "You knuckle-head, of course we thought about advertising. It's right here under ... " It was only through my being okay with that po-tential reaction that I was able to help them.

MAKE DUMB SUGGESTIONS
(Fear of Being Embarrassed)

Naked service providers go beyond merely asking questions that others shy away from; they make suggestions that they aren't sure of, knowing that they are putting themselves in a position to be even more embarrassed.

But as is true for the dumb questions, a client is going to remember that one great idea a consultant proposes far more than the not-so-great ones. And if that client thought we were holding back our ideas out of fear of being humiliated, they would—and should—feel cheated. After all, they're bringing us in and paying us for the objectivity of our thinking, so they expect that some of our suggestions will be less informed than theirs. If we're not putting ourselves on the line and offering everything we have, they would be unwise to trust us or feel loyal to us.

Once we were with a CEO and his CFO at a client site, and they were talking about the next stages in the company's development. As I knew frighteningly little about finance and public markets, I decided that it couldn't hurt to make a suggestion. "What about going public?" I asked. "It seems like other companies usually do that when they reach this point in their growth." I was as shocked as anyone else when the executives looked at each other and said, "Why don't we go public?" Later that year, they did their IPO.

Keep in mind, for every seemingly dumb suggestion that turns out to be insightful, there are plenty that are in fact dumb. But without taking the risk of putting an idea out there, the good ideas will never see the light of day.

CELEBRATE YOUR MISTAKES
(Fear of Being Embarrassed)

Naked service providers don't enjoy being wrong; they just realize that it is an inevitability. And rather than attempting to hide or downplay their errors, they readily call them out and take responsibility for them. Though this may seem counter-intuitive, it actually increases the client's level of trust and loyalty. Clients don't expect perfection from the service providers they hire, but they do expect honesty and transparency. There is no better way to demonstrate this than by acknowledging when a mistake has been made and humbly apologizing for it.

TAKE A BULLET FOR THE CLIENT

(Fear of Feeling Inferior)

This is perhaps the most difficult principle to explain, as it is easily misunderstood and largely counter to what our culture inotillo in uo.

First, the misunderstood part. Taking a bullet does not mean enabling a client to do the wrong thing by blindly and obsequiously absorbing blame for them. It is about finding those moments when we can humble ourselves and sacrificially take some of the burden off of a client in a difficult situation, and then—and this is critical—confront them with the kind truth. Without that confrontation, taking a bullet would indeed be enablement. But there are those moments when a service provider is in a rare position to accept responsibility for something that may or may not have been their fault. And of course, when there is any doubt, taking a bullet means that the consultant always errs on the side of accepting responsibility.

Taking a bullet is countercultural because we are encouraged in life to deflect responsibility for problems, especially if we are not sure that we have done anything to warrant blame. Whether we're siblings fighting over our LEGO sets or plaintiffs in a legal battle, we generally seek to avoid direct or collateral damage in difficult situations. Naked service providers "throw themselves on grenades" for their clients, knowing that the grenades encountered in a business setting are usually not lethal, and that the act of doing so builds extraordinary trust and loyalty. Of course, occasionally grenades are "lethal" in that they destroy the account, but even that is something a naked consultant will accept.

I once worked with a large international client, helping them plan worldwide leadership and strategy conferences. My responsibility included setting the agendas, creating content, and organizing the various activities for the hundred or so executives who attended. During one event, my client became concerned that the event was falling behind schedule and implored me to interrupt the presenters and push them to wrap up their talks. Finally, he poked me in the ribs and said, "Tell him to hurry up!" I turned on the microphone I was carrying and very kindly asked the presenter to finish up in the next five minutes, only to have that presenter unleash on me a few angry and insulting comments in front of a hundred senior executives. I turned to see what my client would say, only to see him disappear out the door to the conference center, leaving me alone to absorb the heat. (I promise you, I couldn't make this up.)

Later, that client acknowledged the uncomfortable situation, although he didn't come right out and apologize. However, he demonstrated his gratitude through his loyalty to me and my firm and his general level of appreciation for everything we did for him. And as awful as that moment was, I came to the conclusion that we had helped him by mitigating a potentially damaging situation for him.

MAKE EVERYTHING ABOUT THE CLIENT
(Fear of Feeling Inferior)

This is another tactic that seems simple and obvious, but it is harder than it seems—and also more powerful. Naked service providers throw their full attention into the world of the client. They do not try to shift attention to themselves and their level of experience or knowledge; rather, they make it clear that their focus is on understanding, honoring, and supporting the business of the client. As a result, naked service providers often downplay their own accomplishments, allowing clients to discover them for themselves. There isn't much more to say about this one, which is as important and difficult as it is simple.

HONOR THE CLIENT'S WORK
(Fear of Feeling Inferior)

Okay, this one sounds a little like the previous one, not to mention motherhood and apple pie, but it's bigger than that. Naked service providers honor the client by taking an active interest in their business and by appreciating the importance of that business to the client and the client's customers. And this can't be faked. Even when a client's business isn't something that a service provider is naturally passionate about, they will find a way to develop and demonstrate an interest out of respect for the client's livelihood.

This begs the question, "What if a potential client is involved in a business that we don't respect?" Not being able to honor that business is a good indication that we shouldn't be doing that work. My firm has been approached by companies involved in a legal business that we nevertheless cannot support from a moral or ethical perspective, and we don't hesitate to kindly pass on those business opportunities. Not only would we be contributing to something we don't want to support, but we would be unable to honor their business.

DO THE DIRTY WORK
(Fear of Feeling Inferior)

Naked service providers are willing to take on whatever a client needs them to do within the context of their services. Sometimes what a client needs isn't as attractive or exciting as we would like. It might cause us to be perceived as lower than the client, or perhaps just lower than we would like to be perceived. But because we are humble and more concerned about our clients than we are about ourselves, we'll do what they need. In doing so, we'll earn their loyalty and gratitude.

A colleague and I once worked with a large international company to help them improve the health of their organization and the capacity of their leaders. Part of that work involved organizing a leadership development conference. In addition to designing curriculum and working with the CEO and other senior executives to help them better inspire leaders, we found ourselves planning dinner menus and running microphones around the room during Q&A sessions.

I remember someone telling me that we shouldn't be doing that because it was beneath us; it made us look like support staff instead of expert advisors. And though that may have been the case in the eyes of the attendees at the conference, we knew that the executives who hired us and worked most closely with us saw it as our complete dedication to them and their organization.

ADMIT YOUR WEAKNESSES AND LIMITATIONS
This principle is perhaps the most general and all-encompassing. It also sounds a lot like celebrating your mistakes, but it differs in a few important ways. First, it is one

thing to be honest about a single mistake, and quite another to admit a general weakness. But the fact is, we all have weaknesses, and if we try to cover them up we'll probably put ourselves in a situation of having to do more and more of what we aren't good at. We'll also wear ourselves out by trying to be something we're not, which not only is exhausting but also prevents us from doing our best in the areas in which we can thrive.

BROADER
APPLICATIONS
OF NAKEDNESS

The principles in this book apply most directly and comprehensively to businesses like management consulting, financial advising, public relations, technical services, and internal corporate support services. However, they can be applied to a variety of other service businesses involving ongoing relationships with clients.

This could certainly include family practice doctors, retained lawyers, sales account managers, life coaches, building contractors, insurance agents, and even personal trainers. And although every principle of naked service may not apply to each of these fields, I think that most of them do, and they can help any service provider inspire loyalty and trust with clients.

Even beyond the world of clients, being naked has its benefits and advantages. When we can demonstrate vulnerability to the people we live and work with, we build stronger relationships, affirm our trust in them, and inspire them to become more vulnerable themselves. And that is certainly worth getting naked for.

ACKNOWLEDGMENTS

irst, I want to thank the many clients I've worked with over the years who have allowed me—and our firm—to be naked. I especially want to thank our earliest clients who helped us practice and get comfortable with the concept of vulnerability. That includes terrific people like Jennifer K. and a bunch of nice folks in Utah; Mark T., Kristen W., Tom C., and others in San Francisco and New York; Alan A. and his team from the East Bay; Jean K. and her crew in the Valley; Ruann E. and her team in the city; and Mark W., Kris H., Gary B., and a long list of others spread here and there. We won't forget the experiences we had with you or the lessons we learned from you.

Of course, I want to thank my "partners in nakedness," my colleagues at The Table Group. Because we try to eat the food we cook, we have had a long history of vulnerability with one another. You are part of my family, something that I don't say easily but mean wholeheartedly. And special gratitude for Tracy and your truly extraordinary dedication to and counsel around this book.

I'm also thankful for the two dozen consulting partners of our firm, people spread around the globe who are nakedly helping organizations become healthier and teams become more cohesive. You have breathed new life into our world at The Table Group, and we appreciate the trust you have placed in us.

I want to give a special thanks to two of our slightly more recent clients and corporate friends—Southwest Airlines and Chick-fil-A—both of whom have made us feel like part of their families and reminded us that work is more than work.

Much thanks go to Jim, my agent, whose willingness to be naked with us has been so important to our firm. And to Rita for your fabulous PR support.

I have to give big thanks to the many wonderful people at Jossey-Bass/Wiley in San Francisco, Hoboken, and Portland, who work so hard to make my little books successful, and who have been with us from the beginning. Special thanks to Susan for your latitude, support, patience, and humor over the years.

I am so thankful for the many people who I've met through my work and church life who have become such dear advisors, mentors, and friends over these past years, Matthew K., Daniel H., Alan H., Randy H., Tom L., John B., and Ken B. I wish I could spend a lot more time with you, and I cherish the minutes we do have together.

I'm grateful for my friends near and far, and the communities that have been or are a part of my life and my formation: St. Isidore parish and school, Garces High School, and Our Lady of Perpetual Help parish and school.

I'm certainly very grateful for my mom and my extended family in California, Mexico, and Colorado, who remain patient with my busy schedule and inability to visit more often. And for my dad, who I miss a lot.

And of course, I reserve so much thanks for my passionate and always supportive wife, Laura, and our sweet and noisy boys, Michael, Casey, Connor, and Matthew. I love you all more than I can say. And yes, I know I say it a lot, but it's still not enough.

Finally, I give thanks for everything and I give all praise and glory to my Lord, God, the Father, Son, and Holy Spirit. I humbly pray that I may use what has been given me to serve You and my neighbor, as You commanded.

ABOUT THE AUTHOR

Patrick Lencioni is founder and president of The Table Group, a firm dedicated to providing organizations with ideas, products, and services that improve teamwork, clarity, and employee engagement.

Lencioni's passion for organizations and teams is reflected in his consulting, speaking, and writing. He is the author of several best-selling books. After eight years in print, his book *The Five Dysfunctions of a Team* continues to be a weekly fixture on national best-seller lists.

When Lencioni is not writing, he consults to CEOs and their executive teams, helping them to become more cohesive within the context of their business strategy. The widespread appeal of Lencioni's leadership models has yielded a diverse base of clients, including a mix of Fortune 500 companies, professional sports organizations, the military, non-profits, universities, and churches.

In addition, Lencioni speaks to thousands of leaders each year at world-class organizations and national conferences. He was cited in the *Wall Street Journal* as one of the most sought-after business speakers in the nation.

Prior to founding his firm, he worked as a corporate executive for Sybase and Oracle and began his career as a management consultant at Bain & Company. He also served on the National Board of Directors for the Make-A-Wish Foundation of America.

Patrick lives in the San Francisco Bay Area with his wife, Laura, and their four sons, Matthew, Connor, Casey, and Michael.

To learn more about Patrick and The Table Group, please visit www.tablegroup.com.

the table group
a patrick lencioni company

The Table Group is dedicated to helping organizations of all kinds function more effectively through better leadership, teamwork, and overall health.

Visit our website, and explore:

Consulting: Table Group Consultants employ the 'naked' approach in all their consulting and training engagements. With a variety of service offerings, all sessions are practical, fast-paced, and application oriented.

Speaking: Patrick Lencioni brings his models on teamwork, leadership, and organizational health to tens of thousands of leaders each year.

Books: Patrick Lencioni's eight best-selling books have sold nearly 3 million copies worldwide and tackle topics surrounding organizational health, leadership, and teams.

Products: The Five Dysfunctions of a Team and The Three Signs of a Miserable Job products were developed to help managers, leaders, and their teams address issues around teamwork and job fulfillment.

www.tablegroup.com   925.299.9700